CREATIVE PARENTING SKILLS

THE TRAINING HANDBOOK

JENNIFER L. WILKE-DEATON, MA, LPA

DEDICATION

To the most inspirational people in my life:

My husband who always has more belief in me than I have in myself

My Grams who taught me what being a good parent could create

Mom and Dad who gave me faith in grown-ups

My father who always pushed me to the next level of success

My sister who always sees me for who I am

Geraldine who does inspire me with a lifetime of experience

& to my niece Meredith who always lets me play Dora on rainy afternoons.

I thank you all.

CREATIVE PARENTING SKILLS

THE TRAINING HANDBOOK

JENNIFER L. WILKE-DEATON, MA, LPA

Eau Claire, Wisconsin

2006

Copyright © 2006 Professional Education Systems Institute

Professional Education Systems Institute, LLC
PO Box 1000
200 Spring Street
Eau Claire, Wisconsin 54702

Printed in the United States of America

ISBN: 0-9749711-7-0

For information on this and other PESI manuals and
audio recordings, please call 800-843-7763 or
visit our website at www.pesi.com

About the Author

Jennifer Wilke-Deaton, MA, LPA, is a clinician in private practice in Mount Sterling, KY. After growing up in the near west suburbs of Chicago, she received her undergraduate degree from Northern Illinois University. She moved to rural Appalachia Kentucky to focus on the treatment of child abuse victims and behaviorally challenged youth. She received her Masters in Clinical Psychology from Morehead State University. Jennifer is a nationally recognized public and keynote speaker and has many years of clinical experience in community mental health, public advocacy, consultation, court expertise, and private practice. She helped create a regional children's crisis stabilization unit, a children's advocacy center, and an intensive after school program for behaviorally challenged youth. Jennifer's expertise is utilized regularly by private/state foster care, social services, schools, universities, psychiatric hospitals, Head Start, in-home therapy programs, disability determinations, courts, and case management services. Jennifer is considered an expert in the areas of positive parent training, child abuse, Posttraumatic Stress Disorder interventions, treatment of behavioral disorders, and attachment issues. She speaks regularly on topics of behavioral issues, child abuse, attachment and bonding, and psychological testing for several regional universities, public radio, newspapers, and for state-based and private agencies around the country. She advocates exhaustively for children and families in her daily practice. Jennifer lives in Richmond, KY, with her husband and family and enjoys gardening, traveling, music, and the fine arts. Jennifer created this parent training program, which has been recognized by the Governor's Commission for the Treatment of Families and Kentucky's Child Protective Services, to serve what she believes is a misunderstood and poorly supported population.

Author's Comments

As a practicing clinician, I hear many complaints and experience a barrage of referrals for children with behavioral problems (many of them not clinically significant). I often experience feelings of frustration with our mental health and educational systems (of which I am a part) on a daily basis. We professionals, along with many exhausted parents, have a common core problem: "How do we help these kids when we feel like we have tried everything?" So often we point the finger of blame at parents and teachers in these children's lives, which leads to a great sense of disempowerment. So how do we help people feel desire, develop drive, and sustain effort when they simply experience failure after failure with these children?

I have some concerns regarding our approaches to parent training and classroom management over the past 15–20 years. One of which is that we seem to be creating secondary gain-driven and poorly centered (self-aware) children who often carry these values into adulthood. We have taken the demand for K.I.S.S. (keep it short and simple) techniques and have unintentionally fueled the development of relatively severe and difficult to stabilize behavioral problems (e.g. Oppositional Defiant Disorder and Conduct Disorder) and perhaps even more rigid personality characteristics.

Firstly, many of the behavioral programs in schools, homes, psychiatric units, detention facilities, and counseling centers are based on obtaining secondary gain (tangible or external rewards). We have developed many different kinds of token economies, point systems, leveling systems, and other behavioral purchasing plans over the past several years (Lieberman, 2000; Ayllon, 1999; Alyord, 1998), which generally work for a short period of time and then ultimately fail or become open to manipulation or "cheating" by the target population. Token economies are actually a fantastic program for daycare, pre-school, and grade school settings, but should only be used to help establish the practice of classroom rules and scheduling. Point systems, which are often utilized in residential settings and therapeutic detention sites, are based on the gains/losses concept of behavioral management. Unfortunately, these types of systems are more often based on losses rather than gains. Earning-based systems are much more effective in developing positive self-esteem and intrinsic desire, but are also very complicated and difficult for parents to manage on a daily basis. It is unfortunate that these types of programs have been divvied out to families and school systems without the proper theoretical understanding and guidance of application. I find that programs like these have excellent intentions, but are generally underdeveloped, over-generalized to a large person-base (rather than individualized), and used as a failing mainstay for the long-term treatment of clinically significant negative behaviors.

A broad concern is that point systems utilize reinforcements (i.e. poker chips, points, rocks, buttons, etc.) that are in no way connected to the behaviors at hand. Research has been very specific about the importance of immediate feedback as a necessity to adjust and develop healthy and efficient cognitions. The process of immediate and relatable feedback can actually help develop and hardwire neural connections in the brain. People using these systems have the basic understanding that feedback must be given to the individual, but what they are missing is that not only does the feedback from the environment need to be immediate but also related to the initiating behavior (Kagan, 2001; Mesulam, 1997; Beatty, 1995; Benton, 1968). For example, how do 100 points earned over several hours or days, used to purchase stickers or balloons from a "store" have anything to do with developing positive communication or self-regulation?

If you know children whose behaviors are being managed by a point system or token economy, you also know that the thought of losing a representative point can frequently provoke anxiety, create lying responses, and even aggressive behaviors (exactly the opposite of what we are trying to achieve). Often, children experience thoughts of "unfairness" or deep loss when participating in systems such as those aforementioned. I also hear comments from clients, such as, "I'm saving up my points to get something really good." Never mind that being trusted, having the respect of people, and not having your movement constantly restricted by others should generally be considered a pretty good thing. By the time children have earned the amount necessary to purchase goods or extra privileges, the importance of the positive behavior that was required to earn the point in the first place is often lost in the process of getting "stuff." This is why I believe we have many children and adolescents saying to us, while holding their hands out, "I'll be good, but what will you give me for it?"

These types of systems of behavioral reward and consequence also rarely have much in common with real-world experiences, such as reciprocal relationships, educational gains, or volunteerism. One of our goals should be to develop behavioral patterns that can be practiced in many places consistently. Generalized and well-practiced behaviors are the longest lasting. (We already experience this with behaviorally problematic children; both positive and negative behaviors can be generalized.) Generally, we adults do not earn tangible rewards for everything that we do. As parents, clinicians, and school staff our focus needs to shift in the direction of developing intrinsic desire for the betterment of the self (doing the "right" thing because it feels good). We must begin to highlight the importance of self-efficacy, positive self-esteem, self-worth, and work ethic. Many of the programs I have had experience with are focused on strict compliance, when at times it is not healthy or safe to "do exactly as we are told the first time (i.e. gang participation, sexual victimization, and substance use/abuse)." This is not to say that we throw out the whole kit and caboodle. It is perfectly appropriate to have some external rewards as a fringe benefit, because it is fun to gain tangible rewards from our world. These types of rewards lose their significance when they are taken for granted as part of daily life.

My second area of concern is that due to the demands for short-term and brief interventions, we clinicians have become more advisors than counsel to our clients. It is our responsibility, and a necessary component of effective and long lasting behavioral treatment, to challenge individuals to create individual solutions to their needs. By removing this component of cognitive challenge, we also remove the opportunity to nurture positive independent thought and effective problem-solving skills. Many of the children and families that I have worked with have been in and out of the revolving door of treatment for years. Several of the families I have helped have a history of successful achievement of their therapeutic goals during the duration of therapy. Often, these people will return to therapy within months or weeks, because they do not know how to independently apply skills or utilize resources without immediate direction from an outside source (i.e. therapist, case manager, school counselor, or social worker). This is likely due to the approach of giving a laundry list of reinforcers and consequences to families and schools, rather than individualizing plans and promoting healthy mistakes, recognition, and recovery.

In my intensive after school program we made a distinction between "coping skills," which are effective de-escalation and prevention tools easily accessed by individuals, and "coping skills-schmoping skills," which are things people have been told they should use but are not necessarily effective for that individual's needs or matching their abilities. For example, for one child "taking deep breaths" or "counting to 10" may be something they do well and can access without a great deal of assistance, but for others these types of skills may be nearly impossible to utilize. Therefore, the goal is to find what works with each person individually and develop those skills specifically, so that they do not require the constant reminder of, "Now what are you supposed to do when you feel angry?" Remember that we all make mistakes, and that these mistakes are a way of identifying areas that need to change.

Also, many of the techniques that we incorporate into behavioral plans are not specific to the environmental factors that are occurring at the time (impacts from home, other classroom disruptions, etc.) For example, Joey has a problem with the use of foul language. Time-out may be effective and appropriate if he initiated the behavior himself, but if the rest of the students in the classroom initiated the use of foul language time-out only serves to isolate Joey rather than develop positive communication in that classroom setting. Time-out as it is being practiced currently by many parents (to be discussed later) is an effective method of removing a child from harming themselves or other people, but does not meet the needs of all behavioral problems in all settings. In fact, the effort of adults should be focused on the prevention of triggering the incident in the first place to avoid punishment, which is often a short-lived solution to the problem. We need to focus on parent-training that teaches the basic concepts and building blocks of individualized positive parenting (and yes, teachers "parent" too). We need to train the concepts and give them the opportunity to practice and gain feedback from professionals and other parents, so that they are able to apply these skills to a multitude of behaviors and settings.

My goal for this *Creative Parenting Skills Handbook* is to assist professionals in their ability to teach, allow the practice of skills, and then trouble-shoot difficulties for anyone working with children that have behavioral concerns (either clinically or not clinically significant). It is important to set a goal for yourself, as a professional, of focusing on empowering the disempowered, reassuring the fearful, and supporting those that need assistance. People working with children also need immediate feedback and feel a sense of self-worth and efficacy when trying and making mistakes. In doing this, you will experience greater openness not only to initial and ongoing treatment, but also to one's comfort in asking for assistance rather than advice if things become difficult. I refer to this as "getting boosters." The following book includes the basic structure of effective parenting, and as the weeks of treatment go on you will find that you develop more positive parenting skills on a more stable base of building blocks. Rather than starting to train parenting late in the process of well-practiced negative behaviors and frustrated parenting, which constitutes an unstable foundation, we should focus on going back to the basics to avoid the constant and frequent repairs. I wish you the best of luck with these individuals and know that you will experience great success.

Introduction

Why is our treatment with children and families failing so miserably? After making the journey from the suburbs of Chicago to rural Appalachia Kentucky, I realized that the needs of parents were basically the same everywhere. I discovered that this parent population was incredibly underserved everywhere that I went, whether urban or rural. Here we were sending children to treatment facilities, psychiatric hospitals, and intensive therapy only to return them to homes that failed within a few short months. I asked myself, "Why is it that we continue to treat the children we work with, without treating the families and homes they are returning to?" It seemed inconceivable that we might be harming the children we treated by setting them up for failure when they were discharged. I had so many parents say to me, "Jen, I don't understand why nothing seems to work to help my child. Can't you give me the answer?"

In my reflection of these types of questions, I realized that they were absolutely right. We, as clinicians, were treating the disease like a medical professional rather than focusing on the system of dysfunction. By gaining this awareness, I decided to stop doing what was *not* working. Through research, observation, and sampling I created this Creative Parenting Program. I have made a concerted effort to help support, educate, and guide parents through the process of positive parenting and empowerment.

Many of the parents we work with are more comfortable with failing than achieving. I could not find a program for parent training that addressed the frustration and confusion associated with positive changes. This program was created to restructure the way parents communicate with their children, identify their own family needs, have a place to appropriately vent, and find answers to questions they didn't realize they had. This parenting program is structured in an 8 week, one hour a week, group session. I have, for the sake of schedules and billing, cut the program down to a 2 hour a week one month group. In doing this, I only experienced more failure with my parents. Likely due to the learning curve and standards for group rapport building, I found that in week 4 of the 8 week course lights turned on for parents. They stopped being angry about failing and became motivated to achieve. Approximately 90% of the families that participated in this parent-training experienced positive growth and long-term parental successes. I continue to hear from these parents, who at times require parenting boosters and answers to questions as their children develop.

Remember that this is an empirically based parenting-skills group. By being flexible—which demands good clinician education of alternative techniques for the basics—and responding to the needs of each group as a separate entity, you experience much greater and long lasting success. That is exactly what our parents are asking for.

What follows is an outline for clinicians, weekly trouble-shooting information, an outline for parents, handouts (intended to be copied for use), examples to utilize, and a graduation certificate.

Before you begin your first week, be sure that you have screened these parents individually, so that you know they are intellectually and emotionally capable of participating in the group. Also be sure to obtain any releases that are to be signed for the court system or social services. Let them know that their behavior and participation may be shared with these people specifically, but only because they gave you permission to do so.

PARENTS' HANDOUTS AND OUTLINE FOR 8 WEEKS:

I. <u>**Week 1: Our First Meeting:**</u>
    A. Introductions
    B. Confidentiality and Group Participation
    C. How were you disciplined as a child? How do you discipline your kids?
    D. **Consistency, Reinforcement, Punishment, and Bribery**
    E. **Time-Out**—Let's make it work!

II. <u>**Week 2: Cooling Down & Prevention:**</u>
    A. Review and Troubleshoot
    B. **Parent's Personal Time-Out**
    C. **Quiet Time**

III. <u>**Week 3: Cycles:**</u>
    A. Review and Troubleshoot
    B. **Cycles**

IV. <u>**Week 4: Changing How We Talk To Each Other:**</u>
    A. Review and Troubleshooting
    B. Words set off our kids!
    C. What should our kids hear? What shouldn't our kids hear?
    D. **Changing Our Triggers**

V. <u>**Week 5: Compromise:**</u>
    A. Review and Troubleshooting
    B. Have you noticed changes in how you and your kids communicate?
    C. **Compromise**
    D. **Steps to Compromise**

VI. <u>**Week 6: Be Aware and Involved:**</u>
    A. Review and Troubleshooting
    B. The importance of extra-curricular activities
    C. Why should you be involved?
    D. **How do we keep track and protect our kids?**

VII. <u>**Week 7: Keeping Up With These Changes:**</u>
    A. Review and Troubleshooting
    B. **Journaling**
    C. **Behavioral Contracting**
    D. **Safe Word**

VIII. <u>**Week 8: Graduation:**</u>

    A. Review changes in the home

    B. What still stumps you?

    C. Discussion

    D. Verbal Quiz

    E. Certificates/Don't forget to get your "Boosters"

Week 1

The Basics of Punishment, Reinforcement, Bribery, and the Effective Use of Time-Out

PARENTING SKILLS-OUTLINE (THERAPIST)

I. <u>Week One: The First Meeting</u>

A. Introductions and address parents' frustrations without allowing a "gripe session" to occur.

B. Discuss confidentiality and group participation expectations.

C. Review parents' discipline history, argument styles, how they were disciplined as children, as well as the ages of the children with which you are working.

D. Introduce Consistency, Reinforcement, Punishment, and Bribery: (Standard for all ages)

    1. Definition of **consistency**: "Always doing the same thing, the same way, every time."

        a. Use applicable examples

        b. Give the timeline for expected change over 30 days.

    2. Definition of **reinforcement**: "A tool to increase a behavior's likelihood of happening."

        a. Note that you can increase negative and positive behaviors alike (grocery store example).

    3. Definition of **punishment**: "A tool that decreases a behavior's likelihood of happening." (Example of non-physical punishment, too)

        a. Note that physical punishment is short lasting and the least effective parenting technique to utilize

            i. Average effect is 3 days of decreased behavior, before negative behaviors return.

        b. Note that reinforcement is more long lasting and effective than punishment.

            i. Average effect is 3 to 4 weeks, and more with consistency.

    4. Definition of **bribery**: "Providing reinforcement before the expected behaviors occur." (Example of court bribery)

        a. Bribery increases the chances that an expected behavior will *not* occur

        b. Bribery is a method of manipulation for children (example: "If you give me a cookie first, then I will clean my room." The room never gets cleaned)

E. Re-introduce Time-out: (most effective for ages 3-12)

    1. The 5 Rules of Time-Out (In handout section). Recognize that for many parents, they do not believe time-out works because it has failed in the past. Note that they haven't followed all the steps, and that is why it hasn't worked *yet.*

        a. *Time-out should occur in a place free from outside stimulation and interruption.*

            i. Effective places:

                a) A specific chair in the kitchen identified by a string (not the same chair they eat in, and sans items on the table).

                b) A doorway in the hallway away from other children, pets, t.v., radio.

            ii. Ineffective places:

                a) Their bedroom (where they have toys and you expect them to sleep)

                b) The middle of the living room

        b. *Never respond to a child in time-out, unless it is a safety issue.*

            i. Remember that reinforcement can come in the form of attention-seeking (hence, attention-seeking behavior)

            ii. You can verbalize minimally, "You are in time-out, and your time does not start until you are quiet."

            iii. If they speak or move from time-out state, *"Your time-out starts over from the beginning again."*

        c. *One minute for every year of age*

            i. Never more than one minute or the child gets overwhelmed and distracted by the time itself, rather than focusing on the behavior causing the discipline

        d. *The adult is not responsible for keeping time in time out*

            i. Effective timers: Because the child does not have to ask continually "Is my time up?" = reinforcement of a negative behavior, set timer and walk away

                a) microwave timer

                b) stove timer

                c) wind-up egg timer

                d) anything that makes a sound at the end

ii. Ineffective timers: Because you can't hear if a child tampers with the time, and it opens the doorway for inconsistency.

        a) parent/child watch (parents get distracted)

        b) wall clock

        c) no timer at all = guessing game

e. *The <u>most important part</u> is processing or "Talking it out" after time-out is over*

    i. *Immediately* following time-out address the child, ask "Why were you in timeout?"

    ii. Allow the child to recall, without answering for them. Three tries, then assist.

    iii. Then ask "What could you do the next time, so you don't have to have time-out?"

    iv. Process every time-out. They know what they *can't* do, now teach them what they *can* do.

TROUBLE-SHOOTING WEEK #1

Many of the parents attending parenting classes for the first time have no idea what to expect when they come to group. I find that by sitting in-the-round and placing myself as a peer rather than a leader helps initiate positive rapport more quickly. Several of the parents I have reviewed with tell me they are embarrassed when they first come to group. I have often provided coffee or small snacks to make the atmosphere more conducive to conversation. The goal is to remove the pointing finger from the face of our parents and essentially say, "I am here for you."

Immediately identify the guidelines for prompt attendance, confidentiality, and your expectations for them in public places. I support the parents in their endeavor to feel accepted by others in the group, but I make it clear that if they discuss names, information, or others' children outside of group, they will be asked to leave. I emphasize the need for everyone's sense of safety and acceptance in the group setting, which also means there will be appropriate language and respectful treatment of all members of the group. Lack of respect is also grounds for removal. This seems a bit uncalled for, but many of these parents act as inappropriately with others as their children do.

One of the best group rapport building tasks you will do on this day is to discuss how everyone was parented. This conversation leads to normalizing and comfort establishment amongst the group members. Do not be surprised when they say, "My parents beat my butt; I don't know why I can't just do it the same way." This is why the section on time-lines and the differences between reinforcement and punishment is vital.

Parents who are referred by the courts or social services are often quite angry with and resentful of "the system" (of which they believe you are a part). I allow these parents to vent briefly, while teaching them to "make the best of a bad situation." As a firm moderator, I have had to refocus several individuals to the goal of helping their child. These folks are less apt to participate, and I make it clear that success comes with group conversation and participation. They are expected to participate, even if only to ask questions or say "I don't get it!"

During this first week, parents regularly discuss their issues with time-out. They often say, "I tried everything, and that time-out really doesn't work." Identify that the kind of time-out they were using may have only been the first 2 or 3 steps, rather than this type of time-out with a processing stage. Emphasize the importance of processing. I tell parents, "Children have so many things they know not to do. Your job is to teach them things they *can* do (not to mention, that a child forgets why they're in time-out 9 out of 10 times)." Also discuss the importance of body position. Be aware that hands on your hips and crossed arms can be perceived as threatening to children. You can role play eye level communication, open body language, and positive eye contact. Recognize that tired or angry eyes also communicate negative feelings to children and others.

This first week will be a tight week for time. You may need a few extra minutes to confirm that everyone knows what they need to practice before they return the following week.

HOMEWORK: Practice the "New and Improved" Time-Out

(With older children: Practice processing information and coming up with
challenging options for adolescents)

HANDOUT #1

The 5 Rules of Time-Out:

1) **Time Out happens in a place with no noise, distractions, or interruptions.**

2) **Never respond to a child in Time-Out (Unless it's a safety issue).**

3) **1 minute for every year your child is old.**

4) **You are not responsible for keeping time in Time-Out.**

5) **Be sure to "Talk it out"**

   a) "Why were you in time-out?"

   b) "What could you do the next time, so you won't have to have time-out?"

Example 1: (Consistency)

Consistency can be considered "Being a person of your word." If you don't follow through on a threat (empty threats) then you are not likely to be taken seriously by your child. This leads to disbelief that you really mean what you are saying.

For Example, you say, "If you do that one more time, you won't be allowed to stay up late." The child continues to misbehave, and you never send them to bed. That is being inconsistent. If you say to your child, "If you hit your brother one more time, you won't be allowed to go to the football game tonight," and then follow through, you have made that experience meaningful for your child.

Don't make threats that will be too difficult for you to follow through on!

Example 2: (Reinforcement)

You can increase negative behaviors as well as positive behaviors.

For example, you tell your child, "If you are good in the grocery store, then I will get you some M&M's." They enter the store and start to misbehave in the fruit section. You say, "Remember, you have to be good to get your treat?" (At that point they should have already lost the reward). They continue to misbehave throughout the store, but suddenly they see the candy at the check-out. They behave well for approximately 10 feet, and you give them their candy. You have essentially rewarded misbehavior throughout the grocery store, because that was the requested behavior from the start. Chances are, the next time they go to the grocery store with you they will misbehave while thinking they know how to get the candy from you.

Remember too, if you try to give them something every time they do what's expected, the child will be less likely to behave the first time you are unable to provide a reward for their behavior. This type of continuous reinforcement causes a belief that they "deserve" something special for every move they make. Partial reinforcement is most effective (i.e. the slot machine effect).

Example 3: (Punishment)

"Why is it that my child doesn't care when I take stuff away from them?"

For example, every time your child misbehaves you take away telephone privileges. That child knows that they will eventually get the telephone rights back, making the punishment un-meaningful. They are likely to return to the former behavior, because they don't recognize the punishment as a true loss.

Physical punishment is not actually connected to the behavior, therefore making that type of punishment un-meaningful too. How many parents have spanked their child for misbehaving, only to have them do the same thing 3 days later? This leads to the belief by parents that "nothing works."

Example 4: (Bribery)

Bribery does not work—you give something with the promise of an expected behavioral return, only to get nothing.

For example, you are on trial for murder. You approach the judge to offer him 1,000,000 dollars for a "not guilty" finding. If you give the judge the money before the trial, he is likely to find you "guilty" and walk away with your money. If you offer, and show, him that you have the money if he finds you "not guilty," he is likely to find you "not guilty" out of the desire to have the money.

Another example, you say, "I'll pay you allowance if you do your chores." The child asks for an advance on the allowance, and you give it to them. They never finish the chores, because they already have what they wanted before having to follow the guidelines for the earned reward.

Never give the reinforcement until *after* the behavior you expect occurs, or it is considered bribery.

Week 2

The Importance of Self-Regulation Through Parent's Personal Time-Out and Quiet Time

PARENTING SKILLS-OUTLINE (THERAPIST)

II. <u>Week Two: Personal De-escalation and Prevention</u>

 A.   Review uses of "new skills" at home – troubleshoot with parents having input as you moderate (this may be as simple as pointing out a missed step or an inconsistency)

 B.   Introduce the **"Parent's Personal Time-Out"**: (Effective with all adults)

  1.   To be used to avoid disciplining when angry or frustrated

  2.   Recognize the importance of this step to avoid unrealistic discipline (Example: "You're grounded for one year.") It teaches children that they can take time away to avoid trouble or "saying something you don't mean."

  3.   **Steps to Parent's Personal Time-out**

   a.   *State to the child "I'm going to take a minute to calm down before I say something I don't mean…this doesn't mean you are getting out of it, I just need a break."*

   b.   *Parent leaves locale of child for deep breaths, bathroom break, cigarette, etc. (Not intended to increase anger by mulling, but to "chill out").*

   c.   *Return to child and state, "I am glad I took that time, because I was able to calm down and think about what I wanted to say to you."*

   d.   *Then discipline realistically*

 C.   Introduce **"Quiet Time"**: The child's version of Personal Time-out (Effective with all ages)

  1.   Opportunity for a child to calm *before* requiring time-out or other discipline.

  2.   Help parents to be aware of children's behaviors as they escalate (can use the escalator metaphor to help with comprehension).

  3.   Note that this is a technique to teach the skill of self-control to the child, and help parents recognize their own short fallings in impulse control.

  4.   **Rules and Steps to Quiet Time:**

   a.   *Not to be used if the child has acted out or been aggressive either physically or verbally. This technique is to be used* before *that occurs.*

   b.   *Identify the escalation without name-calling or labeling the child's behavior ("You seem like you're not feeling well right now . . .").*

   c.   *Offer a quiet space or activity that does not promote increased aggressive behavior to prevent escalation.*

    i.   Effective Quiet Activities:

        a) bedroom with toy

        b) coloring

        c) reading (comics, books, not school work)

        d) playing calmly with pet

    ii. Ineffective Quiet Activities:

        a) video games

        b) loud/angry music

        c) running outside

        d) leaving with friends

   d. *Allow the child to remain in Quiet Area as long as necessary to calm themselves.*

   e. *The child is to return when they are calm for praise ("It's good you were able to do that, because I know that sometimes it seems pretty hard to stop being angry").*

Offer as option in the future, with the parent as a "helper" if needed. (Some parents say they don't think it will work. Ask them to try for two weeks and note the difference in their home environment and interactions with their children).

TROUBLE-SHOOTING WEEK #2

The first activity the group needs to participate in is troubleshooting for the homework from the week before. We tend to give people skills without following up, and wonder why it is they were unsuccessful. You will get questions about how to handle the child when they refuse to go to time-out. I generally tell parents to give a choice to the child. "If you stay in time-out, you're done…If you choose to keep getting out of time-out, then you will lose this privilege." Remind them to tell the child "Time-out doesn't start until you sit down."

Emphasize the importance of being consistent, and not giving up on this skill after it fails one time. You may want to discuss the 30-day improvement time-line that come with consistent effort. Also identify that after week two of consistency children often test limits and try to push parents out of using time-out. They should expect positive and permanent changes (albeit slow) after 30 days.

Behavioral Change With Consistency

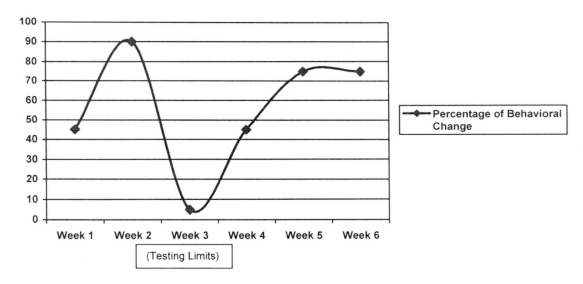

Parents often fail to identify that at times their emotions get in the way of appropriate parenting. Use examples of escalated arguments between adults to highlight the importance of "calming down" before discipline. This is also the best way to avoid the potential of child abuse. Allow parents to discuss times when they have over or under-disciplined because they were not thinking clearly through anger or frustration.

Parents also have difficulty recognizing these same behaviors in their children. They need to be supported to teach their children to calm down before "going off," through the use of Quiet Time (a prevention skill). Also identify that many of their children's behaviors can be learned through observation of their own poor emotional control. The best way to teach children under the age of 12 is to "lead by example." Children learn to generalize observed behaviors much more quickly than trained emotional control skills.

HOMEWORK: Practice Parent's Personal Time-Out and Quiet Time

HANDOUT #2

Steps to a Parent's Personal Time-Out:

1)   Say to your child *"I'm going to take a minute to calm down before I say something I don't mean. This doesn't mean you are getting out of it, I just need a break."*

2)   Leave the area for deep breaths, bathroom break, cigarette, etc.

3)   Return to your child and say, *"I am glad I took that time, because I was able to calm down and think about what I wanted to say to you."*

4)   Discipline realistically.

HANDOUT #3

The Steps to Quiet Time:

!)   Use *before* the child has been verbally or physically aggressive.

2)   Say, *"You seem like you're not feeling well."*

3)   Offer a quiet space and activity.

4)   Let them stay in Quiet Time as long as they need it.

5)   When they return say, *"Its good you were able to do that, because sometimes it's even hard for me to stop being angry."*

6)   Say, *"You can do this again, if you need it."*

Example 5: (Disciplining in times of anger)

You are frustrated with your child for disobeying the rules at school and home (although discipline should always occur in the place the behavior happens—school at school and home at home). When you ask them why they did this they say, "I don't know!" This makes you even more upset. You say, "You are grounded for a year!" (Remember that you have to be consistent, which means you are expected to actually ground them for one year. That will be the longest year of your life). If you had taken the time to cool off by using a Parent's Personal Time-Out, you could have prevented the misery of the next 365 days.

Another example: Many parents who utilize physical discipline often use this approach when angered by their child's behavior. People are more apt to be cruel or aggressive when angry, hurt, or frustrated whether they realize it or not. Physical abuse is a serious charge that can often be substantiated by a small bruise, red mark, or soreness. If you physically punish when you are angry, it increases your chances of inflicting abuse on your child. Is it worth the removal of your child from your home? Or better yet, is it worth the guilt you may feel even if you do not leave marks on your child? Unfortunately, this also teaches children to be aggressive when they are angry. Why is it okay for the parent to be physical, but not the child? This is often perceived by children as a one-way street, and they become confused by the separate standards for behaviors between adults and children.

Week 3

Understanding How Emotions
Work Through Cycles

PARENTING SKILLS-OUTLINE (THERAPIST)

III. <u>Week 3: Cycles</u>

    A. Review uses of "new skills" at home. Troubleshoot with parents.

    B. Re-identify the importance of consistency and follow-through, highlight "choose your battles wisely."

    C. Introduce **"Cycles"**:

        1. All emotions work in cycles, because everything we say and do has an impact on our world (Examples of anger, sadness, happiness. Use visual aid of circle with arrows = meltdown or "going off").

        2. What has a cycle in your home?

        3. Use of washing machine as metaphor for anger cycles

        4. How can you pull out of cycle? (with coping and diffusing techniques)

            a. Use of "apology" to diffuse the trigger (not an apology for discipline, but for creating the negative emotion).

            b. Personal Time-Outs

            c. Quiet Area

            d. Other *individualized* coping skills

        5. Identify that not all coping skills are effective for everyone.

Give other examples that can apply to spousal or occupational relationships (i.e. wake up late to alarm = harried = speeding ticket = verbal aggression with employer. Where could you have pulled out of that cycle?).

TROUBLESHOOTING WEEK #3

During this week's session it is vital to review parents' ability to calm themselves before disciplining. Be sure to point out subtle differences in temperament and how these changes can increase their ability to impact their children in positive ways. You will generally find that by week 3 parents are using concepts of reinforcement much more frequently than punishment. Help parents identify specific experiences of compliance and reference their own mood during these interactions with their child.

This week's session focuses on the concept of emotional cycles. This topic begins to illustrate to parents that even small changes in language, body posturing, and communication can effect how their children respond. The concept of cycles also gives the group an opportunity to understand accountability rather than identifying their child's behavior as "their problem." The use of metaphor is an effective method of teaching this concept (please refer to the example of a washing machine).

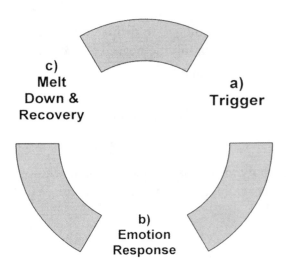

When discussing the concept of triggers/antecedents (a) it's important to note that triggers can be verbal, physical, and non-verbal. Generally, people initiate cycles of emotions through non-verbal and verbal cues before ever being triggered by physical cues (except in cases of persistent physical threat or abuse). Helping parents and teachers recognize that the tone, tempo, and timing of their commentary can lead to escalation is a good first step in helping then comprehend how they impact their child and others.

When identifying emotional responses (b) help parents understand that just because they exhibit anger, sadness, and frustration in certain ways does not mean that their children respond in a like fashion. Often children do not become overt with their emotions until they are near to the point of "meltdown." Therefore, it is helpful to give parents time to reflect on cues their children show before full escalation (e.g. social withdrawal, refusal to speak, poor eye contact, shallow breathing, etc.)

When discussing the concept of meltdown/escalation (c) I often use the concept of a volcano. When one escalates they often affect many areas of their lives (home, school, daycare, work, etc.), not unlike the explosion of a volcano, which damages all of the surroundings. It takes several months or years for the surroundings to recover from the shock of the explosion and begin to develop fertile ground. Escalation is in essence a volcanic eruption that takes everyone by surprise, and takes time to recover from. Therefore, wouldn't it be best to avoid the explosion in the first place? I tell parents that it is very possible to avoid meltdown and recovery time, by altering the antecedents (please use the word trigger, as it is easier for parents to wrap their brains around).

After you have discussed the concept of cycles and offered parents the opportunity to identify their own examples (either with their children or other adults) It is important to discuss healthy ways to assist in de-escalation from an already triggered cycle. Remember that the idea is to explore effective coping skills, not *"coping skills, schmoping skills."*

One generally effective verbal coping skill, or pull-out technique, is an apology. Be careful when discussing this concept, because many parents have the tendency to apologize for discipline. We want to teach them that part of being consistent is that when you parent you do not lose power by backing out of appropriate discipline. Parents already know from week 2 that they will calm themselves before interacting with their child in the role of limit-setter, so there should be many less incidents of improper or unrealistic discipline. Therefore, when apologies are made early in a cycle they should sound like, "I'm sorry you are angry right now" or "I'm sorry you feel like I tried to hurt your feelings." Discuss the importance of less threatening "I" statements, as they are important methods of communicating a successful de-escalation.

Other coping skills you may want to introduce to the parents: 1) Take two or three steps away from each other (proximity) 2) Smile and continue to make positive eye contact (positive non-verbal cues) 3) Sit on the floor and take deep breaths (modeling self-regulation) 4) Selective ignoring (removal of negative attention). These are only examples of areas that may be improved upon, and individual needs and abilities should be taken into consideration. Take time to apply the concept of pulling-out to actual parent examples.

**HOMEWORK: Identify cycles and triggers for the next week
and try to use functional coping mechanisms to "pull out" before meltdown.**

Example 6: (Escalator)

The escalator moves slowly in an upward direction, just as our emotions do. At the bottom of the escalator you have a choice whether to go on it or not. Once you are on the escalator it is difficult to get off, because it works against you moving downward. Imagine each moving step as a step closer to acting out. Many of us can watch our children (and ourselves) "work up or escalate" into a frenzy of bad behavior. At the top, we can get caught in a group of people or have to wait in line to return to the bottom, in the meantime, getting into trouble or hurting ourselves in the fight to de-escalate.

Example 7: (Cycle)

What do you have in your home that has a cycle? A washing machine.

Your washing machine has several settings on it, but the ultimate goal is to have clean clothes. Imagine if you set your machine to clean "whites" and you didn't realize that there was an ink pen in the water. What would happen? Your clothes would be ruined (Can equate with melt down for children, because it takes a lot of effort to clean up the mess that results). If you could get that pen out of the wash before it ruined everything, then you would be preventing a huge mess. You have many options for removal. The best would be to not have the pen in there in the first place, but if you saw it floating while the water filled the first time, you could pull it out without too much hassle. If you couldn't get it then, perhaps you could see it floating when you put the fabric softener in . Maybe then there would only be minor damage. If you allow the cycle to complete, there is little you can do to manage the damage.

This metaphor is not unlike anger (emotion) cycles. A trigger is the starting point and the opportunity to remove the pen is also an opportunity to utilize *functional* coping skills to pull out. Parents enjoy this example, because it is quite visual and they can comprehend the information, rather than speaking the jargon of triggers/antecedents, coping skills, etc.

Example 8: (Alarm Makes You Late For Work)

This is a good example for parents to understand that they too have cycles of anger. It helps them realize that anger is a normal emotion, but what you do with that anger sets you aside from others.

You wake up late, because you set the alarm for p.m. not a.m. You run out of hot water in the shower, because everyone else in the house got to it first. The car started without trouble, Thank God, but you get stuck behind a school bus on your way to work. When you finally get around the bus you race to get to work "only 15 minutes late." Before you turn at your work entrance, a police officer pulls you over for speeding (great!). You are now 45 minutes late for work and your anger cycle started over an hour ago. As you enter the work place your boss makes a comment that your pay will be docked for the tardiness. (This is the point in your cycle that is the most difficult to pull out of, it would have been better if you had called in to say you were going to be late to start with.) In response to your boss' comment you go off and yell. The consequences to that melt down are quite likely getting fired or losing money. Where could you have pulled out of your cycle with a healthy coping skill in order to avoid the mess you are now in?

Week 4

Changing the Way
We Communicate

PARENTING SKILLS-OUTLINE (THERAPIST)

IV. <u>Week 4: Changing Communication</u>

This is usually the week when you see the "lights turn on" for many parents that are truly attempting to use their new skills within their homes.

A. Review uses of "new skills" at home. Troubleshoot with parents.

B. **Introduce Alteration of Verbal Antecedents:** (Effective with all ages)

    1. What sets our kids off more than anything else? (Children usually don't come out punching, they usually start with verbal aggression and escalate into physical aggression, so we need to start there to prevent further escalation).

C. **Identify problems within their homes with verbal interactions:**

    1. Usually begins with arguments immediately following school and work.

        a. Establish with parents the importance of free-time each day after school. (Children have worked a 10 hour day and need a break, too.)

        b. Help them remember that they are now able to identify when their children are escalating.

    2. You will hear: "My kid overreacts to everything that comes out of my mouth."

        a. Identify communication trends within the home.

        b. Question parents as to the communication style of the school staff. (Do they feel overwhelmed at school meetings and parent/teacher conferences? Don't expect any less from their children.)

        c. Identify what type of language they feel is appropriate in the presence of their children.

            i. Foul language

            ii. Name-calling

            iii. Strong emotional language

            iv. Bad-mouthing school staff

            v. Bad-mouthing parents of divorce

        d. Discuss what is, and is not, appropriate to communicate to, and in the presence of, their children (Example of "Your child will do and say what you say and do as their parent").

        e. Identify as a potential trigger/antecedent for cycle

D. **3 Methods to Altering Verbal Antecedents** (Help parents adjust their communication style and ask them how they feel when people do these things to them):

1. ***Don't ever ask a question for which you already know the answer.***

    a. "Did you clean your room?"

    b. "Did you fight at school today?"

    c. "Is your homework done?"

2. ***Do not make requests for behaviors when the child is irritable, upset, or obviously involved in an activity.***

    a. Introduce "Priming the pump"

    b. 1, 2, 3 requests before expected behaviors

    c. Be sure to establish eye contact

    d. Have them repeat your request in their words (Basics of language processing)

3. ***Do not make run-on verbal lists for their behaviors.***

    a. Introduce chore lists (visual cue)

    b. "Doesn't it feel good when you finish a list?"

    c. Identify the appropriate number of chores for different age groups

TROUBLESHOOTING WEEK #4

Generally this tends to be the week when your most resistant and angry parents make a turn around. This will only happen if you as a clinician have maintained a non-judgmental atmosphere with open communication and creative solution gathering. It is quite amazing to see parents enter the fourth week with lights turning on and bells ringing. Prepare yourself for more specific questions during this session.

By this time, many of the group participants are beginning to recognize that what they say and how they behave has a tremendous impact on their child's behavior. Important areas to explore, and also sensitive topics, are: persistent adult arguing in the home, argument styles of the parents (which are often well-modeled to children), and recognizing communication difficulties with the school, social services, or counselors. Taking time to identify these problems and then relating them to the parent's cycled behaviors will aid in empathetic responses to their children.

Of utmost importance is the analysis and gentle changing of language usage (content and context) in the home. Help parents become aware that whatever comes out of their mouths will likely be repeated by their children, regardless of their comprehension of the context. For example, foul language, prejudicial comments, and negative feelings voiced towards school staff or social services will affect whether children are able to appropriately interact with people. I frequently emphasize that what occurs between adults (e.g. IEP meetings, placement planning, disagreements about interventions, etc.) should stay between adults. Children already hear too much adult information as it is, which leads to difficulty understanding roles and recognizing appropriate boundaries.

During this week's group I try to help parents understand that while it is perfectly normal for them not to get along with everyone in their child's life, their children do not have the choice of walking away as an adult would. Essentially, do not create confusion for your children. For example, children must return to school each day and comply with rules and assignments given by their teachers despite how their parents feel about that individual. What children think is, "I'm supposed to do what my teacher says, but my mom hates her, so why bother?"

Revisit cycles briefly and identify that the best case scenario is to actually prevent the cycle from occurring in the first place. The primary trigger for cycles with all people is language. So, how better to prevent escalation than to change the way that we communicate with our children. There are three simple rules to change verbal antecedents and, in return, decrease the frequency of escalations in the home:

1) **Don't ever ask a question for which you already know the answer.** This change is basically teaching parents common courtesy, and through modeling and learned behavior you can successfully teach courtesy to children as well. We adults feel condescended towards when someone asks us a question that we know they already know the answer to. For example, "Did you get that work done?" and the person is looking at your desk with work piled

to the ceiling. Even in adult relationships we do this. "Did you get the oil changed in the car?" despite the fact that the engine exploded on the way to work. We have the tendency to communicate this way with children too. After a parent has walked by a child's very dirty room they ask, "Did you clean your room yet?" Or after a parent gets a phone call from school about their child fighting they ask, "How was school today?" This method of communicating is not only rude, it also sets children up for lying, and then they have two negative things to be disciplined from rather than one.

Parents often do not realize that they set up a system of failure in their homes, and the same holds true for many classrooms. Be honest and straightforward with children and they will learn to do the same. No more tricky "Aha, I caught you in a lie! I can always count on you to lie about the smallest stuff." Of course they lied. Either they don't want to get in trouble for not completing the activity in the first place, or they have no idea what was said to them and they responded based on non-verbal cues.

2)   **Don't ask your child to do something when they are obviously tired, upset, or otherwise occupied**. This is a general Cognitive Behavioral approach that parallels "blocking," a language learning concept. This intervention can potentially save hours of argument over issues such as, "You didn't come to the dinner table right when I told you." No one wants to be told to do something when they are otherwise engaged. And we wonder why children interrupt parents on the telephone or while they are busy with another activity? They learn this from the adults in their lives. With children, this type of interruption is even more of an issue, because if they are involved in some other activity their concentration is not focused on the adult's request. If that is the case, then they will likely not cognitize the information let alone follow through (especially with the ADHD populations).

Priming the pump is a process of:

a)   Making a request for a behavior with established eye contact (wait for a commercial break, time to save a game, etc.) at 10 and 5 minutes before the expected behavior, and again when the behavior is to be initiated (3 pumps).

"You are to come to the dinner table when your program is over."

b)   The child is to repeat the request in their own words (verbal processing) each time the request is made.

Be sure that at the third time you make the statement, "Now it's time to come to the dinner table." This is a statement, not a request. Parents need to remain with the child while they comply, offering assistance if needed. Also, do not expect the child to perform behaviors beyond the initial request (e.g. turn the TV off or put away toys). Parents often complain that this process seems too involved, but it is always important to reference the amount of time they are taking presently to manage escalations and relate that to the less than 3 minutes it takes to complete this activity. Depending upon the child's mood and demeanor, it is possible to remove the repetition component from the second request to avoid triggering a cycle.

3) **<u>Don't make run-on verbal lists for your child to comply with</u>.** A good rule of thumb is that children under the age of 8 should have no more than 3 chores each day (and children as young as 2 or 3 are perfectly capable of picking up their own toys or putting dirty clothes in a basket). From age 8–18 I request that parents limit chores to 5, but the level of difficulty can be adjusted according to age. Use chore lists as non-verbal cues for chores, rather than these overwhelming verbal lists of expectations that parents give children the moment they walk in the door from school.

I explain to parents the importance of recognizing that your children have essentially been "at work" for 8–10 hours already during the day, and it is very important to have free time available after school to recover from the day before completing homework, chores, or other activities.

During this week, you will be pleasantly surprised at how well parents can identify these ways of communicating, and how well they accept these changes. They often say, "Well that makes sense, why haven't I been trying that all along?"

HOMEWORK: Change verbal triggers to avoid escalation.

HANDOUT #4

3 Steps to Changing Our Words:

1) **Don't ever ask a question for which you already know the answer.**

2) **Do not make requests for behaviors when the child is irritable, upset, or obviously involved in an activity.**

3) **Do not make run-on lists for their behaviors.**

Example 9: (Children Follow the Leader)

This example is important to help parents understand that their children do what they do, even without them realizing it.

Do you remember the first word your child said? It is likely they said that, because you stood in front of them for hours at a time saying "mama" or "dada." *Follow the leader.* Do you remember your child trying to wipe the table at age 4, because they wanted to be like you and had watched you for years wipe the table after dinner? *Follow the leader.* Do you remember when your child decided to sneak a cigarette, because even though they watched you cough and choke they wanted to be like you? *Follow the leader.* Do you remember that they hit that kid at school and got suspended, because even though you tell them to behave themselves you always spanked them for being aggressive or having physical altercations with others yourself? *Follow the leader.*

The list goes on, but you get the idea. Help this apply specifically to the problems of your parents in group.

Example 10: (Altering Verbal Antecedents)

How do we change our language within the guidelines for changing verbal antecedents?

Altering Verbal Antecedents

The Old Approach	The New Approach
• "Did you get into a fight today?" • "Is your homework done?" • "I don't care if you're talking to your girlfriend, clean your room!" • "How many times do I have to ask you to take your pills?" • "I don't have time for you right now."	• "The school called about today. Are You okay?" • "What time do you think you can have your homework done by?" • "You can talk on the phone for 10 more minutes, but then it's time to clean your room." • "Here are your pills and a glass of water." • "If you give me 20 minutes, I can pay attention to just you."

Week 5

Introducing Compromise and Developing Flexibility

PARENTING SKILLS-OUTLINE (THERAPIST)

V. <u>Week 5: Compromise</u>

A. Review uses of "new skills" at home. Troubleshoot with parents.

B. Discuss any changes in language that have helped them decrease the occurrence of non-compliance or verbal/physical aggression.

   1. If you only have one person recognize change, you can move along with the strength-based approach for the entire group.

   2. If your parents are having trouble identifying change, use examples from your own practice as a seed for recognition.

C. Introduce Compromise: (Effective with all ages)

   1. Define as a tool to help kids become more flexible thinkers

   2. If children and parents learn to be flexible thinkers together, then they can also learn to respond to changes in their world more easily (rather than "melting down" every time someone or something new occurs—e.g. substitute teachers, divorce/separation, classroom changes).

D. Understanding Compromise:

   1. Identify things parents are unwilling to "give" on.

   2. Recognize that some of those things they may be more willing to "give" on than they think.

      a. Bed time

      b. Eating habits

      c. Curfew (within the guidelines of the law)

   3. Identify things they should not compromise on.

      a. Safety issues

      b. Sex

      c. Legal issues (including tobacco product use)

   4. Establish with parents and children that compromise means "you get *some* of what you want, and your parents get *some* of what they want, but no one gets *every part* of what they want."

   5. Examples of compromise (e.g. Jeremy and Pauline's milk fiasco).

6. Recognize that compromise will actually save time in the end, and help prevent *hours* of arguing and recovering.

E. Steps to Compromise:

1. *The Child **first** identifies what they want.*

2. *Then the parent identifies what they want.*

3. *Discuss what the "middle ground" is.*

4. *Verbalize the final arrangement.*

5. *Shake hands as a **nonverbal contract** (commitment) of the agreement.*

6. *Yes, it is that easy!*

TROUBLESHOOTING WEEK #5

It may seem like smooth sailing in your last few weeks of group, but now is the most important time to go back with your parents and review what is and is not working for them at home. Be sure to revisit the basic building blocks of parenting so that they can conceptualize novel approaches within those guidelines.

During this weeks group the concept of **compromise** is introduced and explained, and it is vital to help parents understand that compromise is not giving in or being inconsistent. This is a truly effective tool to aid in the development of flexible thinking and general cooperation (I find this to be a most important parenting skill for families with severely behaviorally disordered children and youth). In group during this week, I have the tendency to focus on emotional as well as time investments. I often ask parents how many minutes (or hours) they are spending arguing over bedtime, bath time, curfew, etc. This technique can be used for all ages, and aids in the establishment of healthy rapport within the family unit. In other words, by creating a family that talks instead of argues children and adolescents are more apt to access their parents without fearfulness or avoidance.

After reviewing the time wasted arguing, help parents identify where they are mis-investing time and energy that can be better spent enjoying their children. When the group has two or three specific ideas to develop compromises around, discuss the steps to effective and non-manipulated middle ground. Be sure to help parents recognize that there are several areas that should *never* warrant compromise. Anything that can put their child in physical or emotional harm or put them at risk for legal problems should never be up for discussion (e.g. local legally set curfews, drug or alcohol use, physical or verbal aggression, or promiscuity).

Emphasizing that the child makes their request first is vital to this technique's success. Adolescents are likely to be most manipulative in this step. For example, they may choose to stay out on the weekends until 6:00 a.m. If the adolescent identifies their desires first, the parent can balance the scales by saying "Okay, I want you home by 6:00 p.m." If the parent goes first and says, "I want you home by 10:00 p.m." then the middle ground would be 2:00 a.m., which would not be appropriate for a 16-year-old. (See example of compromise)

Go through several examples of compromises to help parents understand that half-way does not mean giving 20–30%, it means 50%. Be sure to teach parents to orally review the arrangement and if needed use visual cues (drawings of how much milk is being agreed upon, using a clock to show bedtime, etc.). In my practice, I tend to use a verbal cue, a visual cue, and a written cue to "make it stick." We also encode and decode information best in sets of 3s. Help parents understand that just because their child says what the compromise is in words, it does not necessarily mean that their child comprehends or processes that information accurately. They may want younger children to paraphrase for clarity (hence, teaching active listening skills).

After the compromise is established it is time for the non-verbal contract. For many generations the handshake has been used as a symbol of trust and "keeping your word." Even very young children comprehend the importance of this gesture. That is why parent and child shake hands after both parties commit to the compromise. This also serves as a neutral reference point if the child does not comply with the agreement. For example, I have many parents that say, "You shook on it, and that means you need to be a person of your word." Often, the child will grudgingly comply while giving themselves an active opportunity to recognize how much less of a hassle it is following through with a commitment, rather than dealing with consequences.

Now is a good time to reference the amount of time parents need to dedicate to the compromise. Usually, it takes less than 5 minutes to come to an agreement, and if the child is asleep by 9:30 p.m. instead of 3:00 a.m., following a meltdown, it can help parents recognize that this is a good investment of time. It may not be the 8:00 p.m. bedtime parents are wanting, but much anger and recovery time is saved in the process.

I sometimes find that parents are slower to identify an opportunity to control the compromise than children and teens are. This means that you may have parents return to the table at a later time wanting to alter compromises that have already been committed to. <u>Do not allow parents to abuse compromise</u>. I tell all of the parents I work with, "Think long and very hard before you decide what you want in the agreement process because once you shake hands you cannot take back your commitment." Another helpful tip for this technique is to use examples in parenting class that can be applied to marriages and other family relationships. When parents learn to identify potential for compromise and their adult relationships, they also become more flexible thinkers in their daily living.

Homework: Compromise on one persistent issue at home.

HANDOUT #5

Steps to Compromise:

1) Your Child *first* identifies what they want.

2) Then the parent identifies what they want.

3) Discuss what is the "middle ground."

4) Verbalize the final arrangement.

5) Shake hands as a *contract*.

Example 11: (Compromise)

Jeremy and his mom, Pauline, fought over a glass of milk for over 6 hours. Why? Because mom was stuck in the "because I said so" mode and Jeremy hated milk, this simple issue gained more power than it should have.

Let's talk about "compromise." Compromise is when you get some of what you want, your child gets some of what he wants, and you meet in the middle. Jeremy understood $\frac{1}{2}$ way, but mom had a harder time with it. Had to give a visual cue in order for her to understand $\frac{1}{2}$ way (chalk board with glasses of milk on it). So Jeremy made a commitment to drink $\frac{1}{2}$ glass of milk and mom agreed that $\frac{1}{2}$ glass was enough. Shook on it, and compliance occurred for several months. Compromise created a system of communication in the home that allowed for flexibility and discussion, rather than simply battling it out (choose your battles wisely). Mom came back 6 months later and said, "I want him to drink 2 glasses of milk now, and he refused to compromise." He knew she was taking advantage of him and abusing the system of compromise. Kids are smart about something as cut and dried as compromise.

Other things that you can use as examples for compromise:

- Amount of food eaten at dinner
- Bedtime
- Homework time
- Telephone time
- Video game use
- Chore Schedules

Week 6

Discussing the Importance of Peer Involvement and Parental Awareness

PARENTING SKILLS-OUTLINE (THERAPIST)

VI. <u>Week 6: Being Aware and Involved</u>

    A. Review uses of "new skills" at home. Troubleshoot with parents.

    B. **Introduce the importance of extra-curricular involvement:** (for social-skill and impulse-control skill development).

        1. Many parents have concerns about transportation and finances. (You can reframe as a "break" for both parents and children.)

        2. Have a list of available resources and activities appropriate for their children's developmental, emotional, and behavioral abilities.

            a. Helpful Contacts:

                i. Schools

                ii. Community centers

                iii. Social services

            b. Good Independent Activities:

                i. Computer classes at school or local university

                ii. Girls/Boys clubs

                iii. Big Brother/Big Sister relationships

                iv. Tennis/Karate

                v. Music (vocal or instrumental)

                vi. After School Programs

            c. Good Group Activities:

                i. Soccer and tennis (non-contact)

                ii. Girl Scouts and Boy Scouts

                iii. Art and Science clubs

                iv. Church Youth Groups/ Sunday School

    C. Emphasize the importance of parents' attendance at anything associated with their child's extra-curricular involvement (If they can't be there because of health, work, or family commitments, help them find one person who can be there).

D. Introduce Monitoring/Positive Communication/Protection Techniques: (Effective with all ages)

1. Establishing curfew and check-in times for all ages.

2. Get to know your children's friends and the homes they enter. (Examples of what can happen if they don't do these things: rape, abuse, neglect, and illicit substance exposure.)

   a. Don't be afraid to appear over-protective or annoying

   b. Helps prevent harm to your children

   c. Shows your children that you are aware of their actions even when they aren't in your home

3. Establish meal times

4. Establish family meetings:

   a. Meetings are an outlet for appropriate expression of frustrations and a problem-solution setting for parents to take an active/helpful role as an authority figure

TROUBLESHOOTING WEEK #6

In this week discussion focuses on the importance for children to be exposed to peers outside the home. Money, transportation, a lack of resources, and limited time are the main reasons parents avoid extracurricular involvement. While it is important that children have unscheduled/free-time, it is also important for them to develop healthy connections outside of the family and school contexts. Extracurricular involvement also offers an excellent opportunity for the development of self-worth, self-efficacy, and positive self-esteem. I urge parents to access resources they didn't know were available. There are many assistance programs and scholarships available for low and middle class socioeconomic families (e.g. schools, social services, churches, and the extracurricular programs themselves).

Extracurricular involvement also does not necessarily mean organized sports or other activities. Many children with behavioral issues have burned up most of the bridges to activities that require group involvement, focus, and a team mentality. Help parents be creative about choices for extracurricular activities. Let them know that their child doesn't have to have on a uniform in order to be involved with peers outside of their home.

Parents need to understand that their power as adults in the home comes from showing appreciation for their child's efforts. Parents say, "No one tells me they appreciate my hard work! Why should I tell them that they did a good job on their chores?" What better chance do parents have to parallel their own anger and hurt to what their children are potentially feeling. These feelings can often be caused by a lack of positive regard by both family members. Often, parents find excuses to avoid attendance to school programs, sports activities, recitals, etc. I ask parents to try to maintain some semblance of appreciation for their children's efforts, while I also recognize that it is difficult to attend 30-40 games in one season. What an excellent opportunity to include other family members in attendance, which also develops a more expansive support system for everyone. Having a healthy support system is vital to helping families function effectively as a team.

This is also the week I urge parents to be more active in their knowledge of where their children are spending time and who their children are spending time with. Long gone are the days of being home at dark. Unfortunately, long gone are the days of parents feeling that they have the right to keep track of their child's behaviors and peer interactions. We have children and teenagers wandering the streets at all hours of the night which is a safety and protection issue. Curfew should be a standard, and phone calls should be made if a child will be late (even if it's only 10 minutes). Parents sometimes consider this a hassle or an infringement on their child's socialization, but reminding them of the world we live in today and what the end result could be, often helps them focus on keeping their child alive and well. If children are to be home after school with a guardian, then they should always check in before leaving the house to play elsewhere. If there is not a guardian at the home, discussion of neglect guidelines through social services should be reviewed with all parents in group.

The parents in these groups also need to be taught to have a safety plan for missing children. The use of safe landmarks and passwords is quite appropriate with children from age 4–18. For example, if a 16-year-old is out with friends and uncomfortable with what their peers are preparing to do, what an excellent opportunity for a password by phone to their parents. If they have to check in any way and a child says, "My friends and I are going to go out to the park, and I was thinking about going and buying some 'bubblegum' before we went." The word "bubblegum" (or any other word) can be a password for the child to communicate discomfort to their parent. Also giving the parent the opportunity to say, "No, I think I want you to come home now" or "Do you need me to come and get you?" When adolescents feel that they can "blame" a lack of peer participation on their parents, this actually creates a healthier belief that their parent will protect them while not losing face in front of peers.

Reminding parents that communication is changing will also help them become more proactive in getting to know their children's friends. Sitting as a family for a meal and helping the family prevent meltdowns with family meetings will also increase a child's belief in their parent to be an "active grown up." Family meetings are vital to helping identify frustrations that are experienced in the home, before having to go off because frustrations have built up without being recognized. The goals of family meetings are not simply to voice frustrations, but to voice concerns appropriately and to be solution-focused. When families communicate more effectively, their children learn they don't need to simply remain upset but that you can actually do something to make it better. Passwords can also be used when someone other than a parent is picking a child up from school or other activities. This passwords identifies that adult as a "safe" person. Therefore, it is important to make the word secret from anyone other than core family members, and those responsible for transportation.

Family meetings should be scheduled regularly at least once a week when starting interventions in the home. I recommend that meetings should last no longer than 20 minutes. The parent always starts the meeting which helps establish appropriate definition between child/adult roles in the home. Children that use foul language and loud vocal tone should still be validated and their frustration should still be reflected by the parent. But remember that it is important to identify healthy ways of communicating frustrations. So following validation, it is important that parents request their child to "try to say the same thing, but in a different way."

There should be no television, radios, video games, or other outside activity occurring during the family meeting. Teaching parents that no one is to get in trouble for "voicing frustrations" is sometimes a difficult task. Having taught parents active listening skills, it is important that you help them also recognize that you can't "listen" if you're talking over your child. Everyone gets an opportunity to speak during family meetings.

In time, the relevance and importance of the topics during family meetings will decrease significantly. This is a positive sign that the family meeting activity is helping parents and children communicate more appropriately, hence avoiding frustrations and meltdowns on a daily basis. Feel free to take a break from family meetings if the only thing that you are talking about is "how smelly dad's socks are." Also teach parents not to be afraid to return to regularly scheduled family meetings if people begin to have difficulty dealing with concerns in the home.

**Homework: At a minimum, establish family meetings
and identify appropriate extracurricular activities for children.**

HANDOUT #6

Tools for Creating Healthy Communication and Protection:

1) **Curfew and Check-In Times**

2) **Know your child's friends and their parents**

3) **Meal Times**

4) **Passwords**

5) **Family Meetings**

Example 12: (What could happen if you don't know their friends?)

Parents refuse to believe that an oversight on their part may have a severe negative impact the lives of their children. Don't be afraid to use the fear component to motivate parents to be more involved and knowledgeable of their children's interactions.

Imagine you sent your child for a sleepover to a friend's house. You haven't met their parents and don't know what the house rules are. Your child may not have a place to sleep, food to eat, water to brush their teeth with, or heat. You would never know, until a social service worker comes to your house to tell you that the children were removed for neglect.

Imagine you sent your 16-year-old daughter to a party at a friend's house. The parents there think its okay to drink alcohol, smoke marijuana, and have boys spend the night. You wake up to a phone call from the Emergency Room, because your daughter was beaten and raped by some drunk boys at the party.

What if you sent your child to a friend's house after school? Those parents regularly use foul language in front of their children, have no curfew, and don't check to make sure where their children are going. You get a phone call that your child was hit by a car on the main road. No one knew where they were or how long to expect them to be gone.

These types of checks are for the protection of children and a parent's sense of well-being and responsibility. This is common sense, but sometimes we feel we are too busy to take the time. How unfortunate would it be to lose your child over 15 minutes of effort not made?

Week 7

Discussing the Importance of Peer Involvement and Parental Awareness

PARENTING SKILLS-OUTLINE (THERAPIST)

VII. <u>**Week 7: Keeping Up with Your Child's Changes**</u>

   A. Review uses of "new skills" at home. Troubleshoot with parents.

   B. **Introduce Journaling:** (Effective with all ages)

      1. Journaling does not have to be pages and pages of written information—in fact the simpler the better (K.I.S.S.).

      2. Journaling should always review what the child has done correctly, even if only minimal progress was achieved. (Examples of small progress monitoring and challenges to meet—e.g. "Today Joe had a hard time talking to more than one person, but tomorrow he plans to talk to Bobby and his teacher.")

      3. Journaling should not be used as a negative record for the child, but as a record of what the parent needs to do to support them.

      4. Types of Journals

   C. **Introduce Behavioral Contracting:** (Effective for all ages, but must be adjusted for age appropriateness) Use visual aide!

      1. Itemize Goals (prioritize and rank).

      2. Identify the importance of daily review/consistent time and place.

      3. Note the importance of "Picking Battles," thus the contract is not to be used as a seed for argument.

      4. Each parent is to create a contract for their child, under the supervision of the therapist. (Construction paper and pens/crayons needed.)

      5. Indicate that the best contract is one that is created with the child present (empowerment).

      6. Practice daily review, challenging language for children, and thoughtful goal support.

   D. **Introduce "Safe Word/Phrase":** (Effective for all ages and interactions with spouses, too).

      1. Define the Safe Word as "A humorous and rarely heard word, that diffuses anger and helps children recognize when they have gone too far." (Examples)

2.   Rules of Safe Word/Phrase:

   a.   The family chooses the word together (You may need to pull ideas from a hat—teaches problem-solving skills).

   b.   To be used only when protecting body or emotions.

   c.   As soon as the word is used "Hands Off."

   d.   If the word is being abused by any party, a new word needs to be chosen.

TROUBLESHOOTING WEEK #7

This is the last week of newly introduced parenting tools and techniques. Depending on the parents and their issues, you can include attachment parenting skills training, positive communication with social services and schools, as well as information regarding medications. During this week group tends to be self-run in regards to troubleshooting current issues in the home.

The three new tools taught this week for parents to learn and incorporate into their daily routine are Journals, Behavior Contracting, and Safe Word/Phrase. Journaling is especially important for foster families, families that have regular contact with authorities, and parents of attachment-issued children. Journals serve as a record of interventions being used as well as their child's response to changes in the home. I recommend that parents take time at the end of each day to jot down progress in areas that could improve. This also helps parents have a reference point to say to themselves, "Wow, 2 months ago we had a lot more problems than we do now."

Journals can also be a tool for parental empowerment and do not require a significantly high reading level. Pictures, simple words, and smiley/frowning faces can represent more than multiple pages of specific notes. After a child and parent have begun communicating more effectively this technique can be a family empowerment tool, allowing everyone to feeling engaged during family meetings.

With higher functioning parents who are able to verbalize and document change, I always recommend that journal entries be dated and have quotations from the child, parent, and other people involved with discipline and reinforcement. This is one method to resolve statements such as, "I never said the 'F-word'" or I don't remember telling you 'I hate you'."

With my behaviorally-disordered youth families I have a standard 3-goal policy. No family should be working on more than 3 goals at a time, and all parties should be focused on progress and strength-based focus on a daily basis. Journals can be an excellent form of identifying goal completion, goal difficulties, and areas that require more cognitive challenge by parent figures. See below.

The format I have found to be most effective and least confusing utilizes a small steno pad with four sections on each page. *(See figure on next page.)*

Section 1, section 2, and section 3 are used to maintain focus on the specific goals being set. The "N" section is used to help families make notes of positive changes in argument styles, exhibited positive communication, mature actions, and generally positive changes in their child's life. Not only is this helpful for parents to refer to when they feel that "everything is falling apart," but this is also helpful for children to be able to recognize that their parents are actually involved and interested in their progress and successes.

Journaling can take less than 10 seconds, and offer a great deal of information about the successes and failures of not only the client, but team members as well. Remember, we are not going to work on the same goals for 6 years without making progress or tracking accountability.

The second tool I like to revisit with parents is the concept of **Behavioral Contracts**. Unfortunately, many behavioral contracts have turned into point systems and token economies with many secondary gain-based reinforcements. Behavioral contracts do not have to be a stress-inducing argument between parents and children. Contracts should be visual or verbal commitments to achieving goals on a daily basis (i.e. completing chores, participating appropriately and family dinners, etc.) Essentially, behavior contracts should identify 3 areas needing improvement. In each of those 3 areas, parents are to focus on challenging their child to do better, rather than focusing on their failures. This is a strength-based model of contracting, and helps develop positive skills for children like problem-solving, proactive choices, and accessing support systems for help when needed. No one is expected to be perfect, least of all parents and staff who are overwhelmed. Children need an opportunity to recognize and change mistakes as they occur. Research has been clear about the positive impact of immediate feedback for developing healthier responses to similar environmental issues. Being preventative, rather than responsive, can actually aid in increasing cognitive development and positive self-esteem.

I ask parents to identify three specific goals that they want to work on each week within the home. Part of challenging language includes reviewing mistakes that have been made in the past and the results that have followed, and helping to choose a more appropriate and proactive selection to "avoid getting into trouble." I often call this "choose your own adventure." I help parents teach children to come up with several options for following through with a goal, and then to identify what results may occur from that "adventure." This allows children to make healthier cognitive connections and process following through with expectations more effectively. Sometimes you need to allow a child/adolescent to explore poor decisions and behaviors to give them an opportunity to experience their mistakes. Remember, it is okay for kids to make mistakes; it's what you do with that knowledge that is the most important. We parents and role models cannot make all the right choices for our youth populations. Think of all the mistakes you have made and how they helped create a more well-rounded and "thinking" individual.

Goal setting for contracts can be relatively simple, and with parents that have never set specific expectations for their children before it is important to start out with basic goals and work your way up. During this week, it is important to help parents recognize how inconsistency can impede progress. Many parents don't understand that telling a child they have done a chore well, and then turning around and "fixing" it because it was not up to their standards, can send mixed messages and create negative self-esteem and poor self-worth. I often spend time with parents defining the capabilities of children at different ages. It can be helpful to define the "best" that a 6-year-old can do and how that is different from the "best" that a 17-year-old can do. Help parents be forgiving of imperfection.

I recommend that for children 15 months to 8 years of age, there should be no more that 3 chore responsibilities (and cleaning your room is 4 or 5 chores in an of itself). For children from 8 years to 18 years there should be 5 consistent responsibilities to complete in the home, depending on the adolescent's cognitive and physical abilities as well.

Goal Setting

Goal #1
I will finish my chores each day

Option #1		Result
I will do one of my 3 chores every 20 minutes until I am done	→	**I could get extra free time**

Option #2		Result
I will do all of my chores before dinner	→	**I might have to eat cold food**

Option #3		Result
I will do my chores tomorrow	→	**I won't be allowed to play video games until I'm done**

This allows the child to make a decision based on their own solutions and identify the strengths and weaknesses of each idea before making a final selection.

The third tool in this week is **Safe Word/Phrase**. This technique is used to re-establish healthy boundaries, develop empathy, and create recognition in children that have difficulty understanding that they have "stepped over the line." It used to be that saying words like "uncle" or "ouch" meant "stop right now, because you won or you hurt me." In today's society those words have lost their power and meaning and therefore we must define boundaries through language. This intervention can help families avoid 3 hour arguments over remote controls or pain caused by play fighting that has gone too far.

The rules of Safe Word/Phrase are quite simple, but can have a tremendous impact on healthy interactions in the home. By creating a new way of communicating, you also create a new way of understanding in the home.

Rules of Safe Word/Phrase:

1)   The word must be outside the context of normal conversation

2)   The word must be humorous

3)   The word cannot be abused or it loses its power

This means that family names, pet names, words like "and" or "the," and any other word that is used regularly in the home should not be chosen. I have some families that have used "pineapple upside down cake" and "ladybug" to define their safety. Words should be humorous because not only does that distract from the "heat of the moment," but it also affects the brain in positive ways. Humor can decrease an individual's sensitivity to change. In effect, it is a sly form of regulation that can pull people further away from the "fight or flight" response to their environment. Most importantly, if families use the word when not experiencing something potentially emotionally or physically harmful, then the word loses its meaning and power. That means that a child cannot use the Safe Word/Phrase if they want to get their way, take toys or possessions from others, or manipulate parents.

Parents are infamous about misusing this technique. If a parent is tired or frustrated the best option is to utilize the skill of Parent's Personal Time Out to prevent saying or doing something they don't mean, rather than using the Safe Word/Phrase to "get them out of my hair." Children will learn to use Safe Word/Phrase to their benefit if a parent teaches them that it can give them false control. If this technique is mistreated the following should happen:

What to do if "Word Abuse" occurs:

1st time = Reminder of the power of the word

2nd time = New word is identified

3rd time = Safe word cannot be used

It is possible for some home to be incapable of using this technique, and that does not mean a complete failure of the system. It simply means that boundaries may be an area that requires more focus in treatment than other areas. I find this to be especially true in households that have children with attachment issues, as these children tend to shatter and abuse boundaries than most other populations. Remember that children that have poor boundaries may also have parents with poor limits and inconsistency (i.e. their own attachment issues).

Homework: Establish a journal, use contracts where appropriate, and create a Safe Word/Phrase.

Week 8

The Final Session

PARENTING SKILLS-OUTLINE (THERAPIST)

VIII. <u>**Week 8: Graduation**</u>

    A. Review uses of "new skills" at home - troubleshoot with parents.

    B. Identify difficulties with communication, monitoring tools, and review efficacy of contracts.

    C. Identify problem areas of parenting for each set of parents (Allow the group to problem-solve together, for added support).

    D. Orally Quiz parents (specifically in problem areas for the group).

    E. Praise and Constructive Criticism.

    F. Give Certificate of Completion.

    G. Remember to offer "Boosters."

TROUBLESHOOTING WEEK #8

This is a week of praise and recognition for parents, and they deserve it! During this week don't forget to troubleshoot new skills in the home. Parents may need some special time to resolve concerns about challenging language and contracting. Allow the rest of the group to brainstorm and role play some of the more basic interactions.

During this week I also help parents understand that they are capable of using these skills in their home long after they attend group. Many parents will ask me "how long" they should use techniques. I usually tell them "forever." I often use the example of chronic dieters. Those people that gain weight and can lose it with diet and exercise, but always return to their old habits when they lose the amount of weight they wanted to lose. The problem with this mentality is that you constantly struggle with weight gain and loss, and never achieve stability. Stability for chronic dieters only happens when they change their lifestyle, and make all those good habits a part of everyday living.

Positive parenting is a very similar concept. If you only use good parenting skills when the going gets rough, then you are more likely to have to return to counseling or group treatment over and over again. If parents incorporate these new skills into their everyday living, then their own behaviors become habit in a good way. By maintaining consistency all the time, not just when things are bad, you teach your children that you are reliable, predictable, and trustworthy. This belief by your children can only foster healthy communication in the home, respectful treatment, and healthy adult lives. I teach all parents that come to group or family counseling that "This is a lifestyle change, not an antibiotic."

Have questions prepared for group this day that focus on the specific difficulties of that group. Maybe this group had a hard time with the idea of flexible thinking, whereas another group may have had trouble getting off the ground with the differences between reinforcement and bribery. Focus the closing "Quiz" questions on those areas.

Remind parents that the goal is for them to be successful all on their own, but if they have forgotten how to handle something or need a reminder of developmentally appropriate changes, they can access you for boosters. I have a standard rule for "Parenting Boosters": If any one parent calls for boosters more than 3 times in one month then they may need to return for some one-on-one intervention, or return for another group. Parents that have the tendency to call more frequently, usually lack the self-efficacy to follow through at home. Having them return as a veteran to group can help develop positive self-esteem when they find that they are actually the more knowledgeable person in the group setting.

Don't forget to hand out certificates of completion for all parents. Some parents throw them away, but others use them as a reminder that they are capable of following through. I also tend to give out certificates to parents because it decreases the necessity for me to have to write letters to courts and lawyers about attendance and participation. As always, be sure to have the appropriate releases for all members of group.

Congratulations to you too! You have successfully completed a rather intense 8-week parent program!

Parenting Clinic Diploma

This certificate recognizes that

_____

Name

successfully participated in and completed

___ / 8 *Parent Skills Training classes*

on this date: _____

Date

_____

Signature of Trainer

References

AACAP (2002). Practice parameter for the prevention and management of aggressive behavior in child and adolescent psychiatric institutions, with special reference to seclusion and restraints. *Child and Adolescent Psychiatry, 41* (2S), 4S–25S. Practice Parameter Statement by the American Academy of Child and Adolescent Psychiatry.

ABIDIN, R. R. (1983) *Parenting Stress Index—Manual.* Virginia: Pediatric Psychology Press.

ABIKOFF, H., HECHTMAN, L., & KLEIN, R. G., et al. (2004). Adding psychosocial therapy to methylphenidate may not improve its effectiveness in stimulant responsive children with ADHD. *Journal of the American Academy of Child & Adolescent Psychiatry, 43,* 802–811.

AGGLETON, J. P. (2000). *The amygdala: a functional analysis.* Oxford, UK: Oxford University Press.

ALEXANDER, J. F. & PARSONS, B. V. (1982) *Functional Family Therapy.* California: Brooks Cole.

ALLESANDRI, M. (2005). *The Social Deficit in Autism: Focus on Joint Attention.* Rev Neurology.

AMATO, P. R. & KEITH, B. (1991) Parental divorce and the well-being of children: A meta-analysis. *Psychological Bulletin, 110,* 26–46.

AMEN, D. G. (2001). *Healing ADD: The breakthrough program that allows to see and heal the six types of ADD.* New York: G.P. Putnam's Sons.

AMERICAN PSYCHIATRIC ASSOCIATION (1998). *Diagnostic and Statistical Manual of Mental Disorders* (DSM-IV), 4th Edition. Washington DC; APA.

AMINGER, G. P., PAPE, S., ROCK, D., ROBERTS, S., SQUIRES-WHEELER, E., KESTEMBAUM, C. & ERLENMEYER-KIMLING, L. (2000). The New York High-Risk Project: Comorbidity for Axis I Disorders Is Preceded by Childhood Behavioral Disturbance. *Journal of Nervous & Mental Disease, 188* (11), 751–756.

AMINI, F., LANNON, R. & LEWIS, T. (2001). *A general theory of love.* New York: Vintage.

ANDERSON, C. J. (2006). Visual Scanning and Pupillary Responses in Young Children with Autism Spectrum Disorder. *Journal of Clinical and Experimental Neuropsychology, Volume 28, Number 7.*

ANDERSON, C. A. & BUSHMAN, B. J. (2001). Effects of violent games on aggressive behavior, aggressive cognition, aggressive affect, physiological arousal, and prosocial behavior: a meta-analytic review of the scientific literature. *Psychological Science, 12,* 353–358.

ANDERSON, R. & PICHERT, J. (1978). Recall of previously inrecallable information following a shift in perspective. *Journal of Verbal Learning and Verbal Behavior, 17* (1), 12.

ANTONY, M., et al (2000) *The Shyness and Social Anxiety Workbook: Proven Techniques for Overcoming Your Fears.* New Harbinger Publications, Oakland, CA.

AREHART-TREICHEL, M. (2006). Increasing Use of CBT Suggests Promising Future. *Psychiatric News. Volume 41, Number 3,* page 21.

ARTZ, S., NICHOLSON, D., HALSATT, E. & LARKE, S. (2001). *Guide for needs assessment for youth.* Victoria, B.C.: University of Victoria Child and Youth Care.

ARYA, S. (1989). In nutrition in mother-child dyad. *Indian Journal of Clinical Psychology, 16,* 34–40.

ASMUDSON, G.J. (2006). *Strategies for managing symptoms of anxiety. Vol. 6, No. 2,* Pages 213–222.

ATTWOOD T. (2002) Frameworks for behavioural interventions. *Child and Adolescent Psychiatric Clinics of North America.* 12.

ATTWOOD, T. (1998). *Asperger's Syndrome: A guide for parents and professionals.* New York: Jessica Kingsley Publishers.

AKSHOOMOFF, N. (2005). *The Neuropsychology of Autistic Spectrum Disorders. Vol. 27, No. 3,* Pages 307–310.

AYLLON, T., LAYMAN, D. & KANDEL, H. J. (1975). A behavioral-educational alternative to drug control of hyperactive children. *Journal of Applied Behavioral Analysis, 8:* 137–146.

AYRES, J. A. (1979). *Sensory integration and the child.* Los Angeles: Western Psychological Services.

BACK, A. (1999). *Prisoners of hate: the cognitive basis of anger, hostility, and violence.* New York: Harper Collins.

BAER, R. (2003). Mindfulness Training as a Clinical Intervention: A Conceptual and Empirical Review. *Clinical Psychology: Science and Practice 10* (2), 125–143.

BALL, G. G. (1993). Modifying the behavior of the violent patients. *Psychiatric Quarterly (historical archive), 64* (4), 359–369.

BALTODONO, H. M., MATHUR, S. R. & RUTHERFORD, R. B. (2005). Transition of Incarcerated Youth with Disabilities across Systems and into Adulthood. *Exceptionality, 13* (2), 103–124.

BANDURA, A. (1984). Exercise of personal agency through the self-efficacy mechanism. In *Self-Efficacy: Thought Control of Action* (Eds.) R. Schwartzer. Washington, DC: Hemisphere Publishing Company.

BARLOW, D. H. (2004). *Anxiety and Its Disorders: The Nature and Treatment of Anxiety and Panic.* Guilford Press.

BARLOW, D. H., et al (1996). Cognitive processing in children: Relation to anxiety and family influences. *Journal of Clinical Child Psychology .Vol. 25, No. 2,* Pages 170–176.

BATH, H. (1994). The physical restraint of children: Is it therapeutic? *American Journal of Orthopsychiatry, 64* (1), 40–49.

BEATTY, W. (1999). *The biology of violence.* San Francisco: West Ed.

BECK, A.T. (2005). *Anxiety Disorders and Phobias: A Cognitive Perspective.* Jackson, TN: Basic Books.

BECK, A.T. (1997). The past and future of cognitive therapy. *Journal of Psychotherapy and Practice,* 6:276–284.

BEDELL, J. R. & ARCHER, R. P. (1980). Peer managed token economies: evaluation and description. *Journal of Clinical Psychology, 36* (3), 716–722.

BELKE, E., MEYER, A. S. & DAMIAN, M. F. (2005). Refractory effects and picture naming as assessed in a semantic blocking paradigm. *The Quarterly Journal of Experimental Psychology: Section A, 58* (4), 667–692.

BENARD, B. (2004). Resiliency: *What We Have Learned.* San Francisco: West Ed.

BENDER, E. (2004). PTSD, Other Disorders Evident in Kids Who Witnessed Domestic Violence. *Psychiatric News, 39* (11).

BENTON, A. L. (1968). Differential behavioral effects in frontal lobe disease, *Neuropsychologia, 6,* 53–60.

BERNE, E. (1961). *Transactional Analysis in Psychotherapy.* New York: Grove Press, Inc.

BERNSTEIN, N. (1996) *Treating the Unmanageable Adolescent: A Guide to Oppositional Defiant and Conduct Disorders.* New Jersey: Aronson.

BEAUCHINE, T. P., KATKIN, E. S., STRESSBERG, Z. & SNARR, J. (2001). Disinhibitory psychopathology and male adolescents: Discriminating conduct disorder from attention-deficit/hyperactivity disorder through concurrent assessment of multiple autonomic states. *Journal of the American Academy of Child & Adolescent Psychiatry, 40* (10), 1222–1230.

BIELING, P. J. (2004). Is perfectionism good, bad, or both? Examining models of the perfectionism construct. *Personality and Individual Differences, 2004.* Elsevier Science.

BLUESTONE, H. (2004). *Youth violence; prevention, intervention, and social policy.* Washington, DC: American Psychiatric Publishing.

BORNSTEIN, R. & PITTMAN, T. (1992). *Perception without awareness: Cognitive, clinical, and social perspectives.* New York: Guilford Press.

BOUDEWYN, A. C. & LEIM, J. H. (2004). Childhood sexual abuse as a precursor to depression and self-destructive behavior and adulthood. *Journal of Traumatic Stress, 8* (3), 445–459.

BOULTON, M. J., TRUEMAN, M., CHAU, C., WHITEHEAD, C. & AMATAYA, K. (1999) Concurrent and longitudinal links between friendship and peer victimization: Implications for befriending interventions. *Journal of Adolescence, 22,* 461–466.

BRADFIELD, R. H. (1970) *Behavior modification: The human effort.* San Francisco, CA: Dimensions Publishing Company.

BRADLEY, S. (2000). *Affect regulation and the development of psychopathology.* New York: Guilford Press.

BRENDTRO, L., NESS, A. & MITCHELL, M. (2001). *No disposable kids.* Longmont, CO: Sopris West.

BRENDTRO, L., BROKENLEG, M., & VAN BOCKERN, S. (2002). *Reclaiming Youth at Risk: Our hope for the future.* Bloomington, IN: National Educational Service.

BRENDTRO, L., BROKENLEG, M. & VAN BOCKERN, S. (2004). The resilience code. *Reclaiming Children and Youth, 12* (4), 194–200.

BRENDTRO, L. & SHAHBAZIAN, M. (2004). *Troubled children and youth: Turning problems into opportunities.* Champaign, IL: Research Press.

BRONFENBRENNER, U. (1979). *The ecology of human development.* Cambridge: Harvard University Press.

BURKE, J. D., LOEBER, R., LAHEY, B. B. & RATHOUZ, P. J. (2005). Developmental transitions among affected and behavioral disorders and adolescent boys. *Journal of Child Psychology and Psychiatry, 46* (11), 1200.

BUSCH, A. B. & SHORE, M. F. (2000). Seclusion and Restraint: a Review of Recent Literature. *Harvard Review of Psychiatry, 8* (5) 261–270.

BUSHMAN, B. J. & HEUSMANN, L. R. (2001). *Effects of televised violence on aggression.* In D. Singer & J. Singer (Eds.), Handbook of Children and the Media. Thousand Oaks, CA: Sage Publications.

BUSSING, R., ZIMA, B. T. & BELIN, T. R. (1988). Differential access to care for children with ADHD and special-education programs. *Psychiatric Services, 49,* 1226–1229.

CANFIELD, J., HANSEN, M. V., HANSEN, P., & DUNLAP, I. (1999). *Chicken Soup for the Preteen Soul.* Deerfield Beach, FL: Health Communications, Inc.

CANFIELD, J., HANSEN, M. V., & KIRBERGER, K. (2000). *Chicken Soup for the Teenage Soul III.* Deerfield Beach, FL: Health Communications, Inc.

CASHELL, M. L. (2002) Child and Adolescent Psychological Assessment: Current Clinical Practices and the Impact of Managed-Care. *Professional Psychology: Research and Practice, 33* (5), 446–453.

CASTLE, S. E. (1996). *Personal Communication.*

CHAKRABARTI, S. et al (2005). Prevalence of developmental disorders in preschool children: confirmation of high prevalence. *American Journal of Psychiatry.*

CHAMBERLAIN, P. (2003). *Treating chronic juvenile offenders: advances made through the Oregon multidimensional treatment foster care model.* Washington, DC: American Psychological Association.

CHARD, K. M., WEAVER, T. L. & RESICK, P. A. (1997). Adapting cognitive processing therapy for child sexual abuse survivors. *Cognitive and Behavioral Practice, 4,* 31–52

CLARK, L. (1996). *S.O.S. For Parenting: A practical guide for handling everyday behavior problems* (Second Edition). Bowling Green, KY: Parents Press.

CLARK, L. (1998). *S.O.S. Help for Emotions: Managing anxiety, anger, and depression.* Bowling Green, KY: Parents Press.

COLE, P. M., ZAHN-WAXLER, C., FOX, N. A., USHER, B. A. & WELSH, J. D. (1996). Individual differences and emotion regulation and behavior problems and preschool children. *Journal of Abnormal Psychology, 105* (4), 518–529.

CONDON, W. S. (1985). *Sound-film microanalysis: A means of correlating brain and behavior.* In F. Duffy & N. Geschwind (Eds.), Dyslexia: A neuro-scientific approach to clinical evaluation. Boston: Little, Brown.

CONDUCT PROBLEMS PREVENTION RESEARCH PROGRAM. (1992) A developmental and clinical model for the prevention of conduct disorder. *Developmental Psychopathology, 4,* 509–527.

CONNOR, D. F. (2002). Preschool Attention Deficit Hyperactivity Disorder: a Review of Prevalence, Diagnosis, Neurobiology, and Stimulant Treatment. *Journal of Developmental & Behavioral Pediatrics, 23* (0), S1–S9.

CONTI-RAMSDEN, G., BOTTING, N. & DURKIN, K. (2008). Parental Perspectives During the Transition to Adulthood of Adolescents With a History of Specific Language Impairment (SLI). *Journal of Speech, Language, and Hearing Research, 51,* 84–96.

CORRIGAN, P. W. (1991). Strategies that overcome barriers to token economies in community programs for severe mentally ill youth. *Community Mental Health Journal, 27* (1), 17–30.

COSTELLO, E. J., MUSTILLO, S., ERKANLI, A, KEELER, G. & ANGOLED, A. (2003). Prevalence and development of psychiatric disorders in childhood and adolescence. *Archived General Psychiatry, 60,* 837–844.

COTTON, N. U., RESNICK, D. C., BROWNE, S. L., MARTIN, D. R., MCCARRAHER, J. & WOODS, J. (1994). Aggression and Fighting Behavior among African-American Adolescents: Individual and Family Factors. *American Journal of Public Health, 84,* 618–622.

CRICK, N. R. & DODGE, K. A. (1996) Social information processing mechanisms in reactive and proactive aggression. *Child Development, 67,* 993–1002.

CRISPINO, L., et al (1984). Cerebellum mediates modality-specific modulation of sensory responses of midbrain and forebrain in rats. Proceedings: National Academy of Science—*Neurobiology, 81,* 2917–2920.

CUNNINGHAM, C.E. (2004) Behavioral and emotional adjustment, family functioning, academic performance, and social relationships in children with selective mutism. *Journal of Child Psychology and Psychiatry, 45* (8), 1363–1372.

CURRIE, J. & THOMAS, D. (1995). Does Head Start Make a Difference? *American Economic Review, 85* (3), 341–364.

DAY, D. M. (2002). Examination therapeutic utility of restraints and seclusion with children and youth: The role of fear he and research and practice. *American Journal of Orthopsychiatry, 72* (2), 266–278.

DE BILDT, A., et al (2005). Social skills in children with intellectual disabilities with and without autism. *Journal of Intellectual Disability Research 49* (5), 317–328.

DIGIACOMO, J. N. & ROSEN, H. (1978). The role of physical restraint in the treatment of psychiatric illness. *Journal of Clinical Psychiatry, 39* (3), 228–232.

DISHION, T. J., NELSON, S. E. & YASUI, M. (2005). Predicting Early Adolescence Gang Involvement from Middle School Adaptation. *Journal of Clinical Child & Adolescent Psychology, 34* (1), 62–73.

DOSREIS, S., ZITO, J. M., SAFER, D. J., GARDNER, J. F. & PUCCIA, K. B. (2005). Multiple Psychotropic Medication Use for Youths: A 2-State Comparison. *Journal of Child and Adolescent Psychopharmacology, 15* (1), 68–77.

DODGE, K. & SOMBERG, D. (1987). Hostile attribution biases among aggressive boys are exacerbated under conditions of threat to the self. *Child Development, 58,* 213–234.

DRISKO, J. W. (1981). Therapeutic use of physical restraint. *Child and Youth Care Forum, 10* (4), 318–328.

DUMAS, J. E. (1989) Treating antisocial behavior in children: Child and family approaches. *Clinical Psychology Review, 9,* 197–222.

ENGLE, P. L. & RICCIUTI, H. (1996). Psycho-social aspects of care and nutrition. *Food and Nutrition Bulletin Supplement, 14* (3), 201–220.

ERON, L. & HUESMAN, L. R. (1986). *Television and the Aggressive Child: a Cross-National Comparison.* Hillsdale, NJ: Earlbaum Associates.

FEIN, D., et al (2005). Pervasive Developmental Disorder can develop into ADHD: Case Illustrations. *Journal of Autism Dev Dis, 35:* 525–534.

FOUSE, B. (2004). Creating a Win-Win IEP For Students with Autism, 2nd Edition.

FRICK, P. J., LAHEY, B. B., LOEBER, R., STOUTHAMER-LOEBER, M., M. A. G. & HANSON, K. (1992) Familial risk factors to oppositional defiant disorder and conduct disorder: Parental psychopathology and maternal parenting. *Journal of Consulting and Clinical Psychology, 60,* 49–55.

FRICK, P. J. *Family Dysfunction and the Disruptive Behavior Disorders: A Review of Recent Empirical Findings.* In: OLLENDICK, T.H. & PRINZ, R.J., editors. Advances in Child Clinical Psychology. (1994) New York: Plenum: pp203–222.

FRICK, P. J. (2000). A comprehensive and individualized treatment approach for children and adolescents with conduct disorders. *Cognitive and Behavioral Practice, 7,* 30–37.

FRICK, P. (2001) Effective interventions for children and adolescents with conduct disorder. *Canadian Journal of Psychiatry, 46.*

FRIEDMAN, S. (1994) *Staying simple, staying focused: Time-effective consultations with children and families.* In: HOYT, M. (Ed.) Constructive Therapies (pp 217–250). New York: Guilford.

GALLER, J. R. & RAMSEY, F. (1985). The influence of early malnutrition on subsequent behavioral development: VI the role of the microenvironment of the household. *Nutrition and Behavior, 2,* 161–173.

GARDENER, W., KELLEHER, K. & PAJER, K. (2002). Multidimensional Adaptive Testing for Mental Health Problems in Primary Care. *Medical Care, 40* (9), 812–823.

GENDREAU, P., LITTLE, T., & GROGGIN, C. (1996). A Meta-Analysis of the Predictors of Adult Offender Recidivism: What Works! *Criminology, 34,* 575–607.

GENDREAU, P. & ROSS, R. R. (1987). Revivification of Rehabilitation: Evidence from the 1980's. *Justice Quarterly, 4,* 349–407.

GIBBS, J. (2003). Equipping youth with mature moral judgment. *Reclaiming Children and Youth, 12* (3), 149–154.

GIFFORD-SMITH, M., DODGE, K.A., DISHION, T. J. & MCCORD, J. (2005). Peer Influence in Children and Adolescents: Crossing the Bridge from Developmental to Intervention Science. *Journal of Abnormal Child Psychology, 33* (3), 255–265.

GLENN, M. (2002). A Differential Diagnostic Approach to the Pharmacological Treatment of Cognitive, Behavioral, and Affective Disorders after Traumatic Brain Injury. *Journal of Head Trauma Rehabilitation, 17* (4), 273–283.

GOLD, M. (1995) Charting a course: Promise and prospects for alternative schools. *Journal of Emotional and Behavioral Problems, 3* (4), 8–11.

GOLD, M., & OSGOOD, D. W. (1992). *Personality and peer influence in juvenile corrections.* Westport, CT: Greenwood Press.

GOLDMAN, L. R., et al (2000). Chemicals in the environment and developmental toxicity to children: A public health and policy perspective. Environmental Health Perspectives. 108 Sup. 3: 443–8.

GOLDSTEIN, A. P. (1999). *Low level of aggression: First steps on the ladder to violence.* Champaign, IL. Research Press.

GOWDY, V. B. (1996). Historical Perspective. In D. L. McKenzie & E. E. Hebert (Eds.), *Correctional Boot Camps: a Tough Intermediate Sanction.* Washington, DC: National Institute of Justice.

GREENE, R. W. (2001) *The Explosive Child: A New Approach for Understanding and Helping Easily Frustrated, "Chronically Inflexible" Children* (2nd ed.) New York: Harper Collins.

GREENFIELD, P. M. (1984). *Mind and media: the effects of television, computers and video games.* London: Fontana.

GREENSPAN, S. I. (1998). The Child with Special Needs: Intellectual and Emotional Growth. Reading, MA: Addison Wesley Longman.

GROVES, D., ZUCKERMAN, D., MARANS, S. & COHEN, D. (1993). Silent victims: Children who witness violence. *Journal of the American Medical Association, 269,* 262–264.

GUERRA, N. G., HUESMAN, L. R. & SPINDLER, A. J. (2003). Community violence exposure, social cognition, and aggression among urban elementary-schoolchildren. *Child Development, 74* (5), 1507–1522.

HAGEDORN, J. M. (1995) *Forsaking Our Children: Bureaucracy and reform in the child welfare system.* Chicago: Lakeview Press.

HEALY, J. (1984). *Endangered Minds: Why Our Children Don't Think.* Simon & Shuster, New York.

HERPERTZ, S. C., MUELLER, B., WENNING, B., QUNAIBI, M., LICHTERFIELD, C. & HERPERTZ-DAHLMAN, B. (2003). Autonomic responses and boys with Externalizing disorders. *Journal of Neural Transmission, 110* (10), 1181–1195.

HEWITT & FLETT (1991). Perfectionism in the self and social contexts: conceptualization, assessment, and association with psychopathology. *Journal of Pers Soc Psychol. Mar; 60* (3): 456–70.

HO, P. T., KELLER, J. L., BERG, A. L., CARGAN, A. L. & HADDAD, J. (1999). Pervasive Developmental Delay in Children Presenting As Possible Hearing Loss. *Laryngoscope, 109* (1), 129–135.

HOBBS, N. (1975) *The Futures of Children.* San Francisco, CA: Jossey-Bass Limited.

HOLTON, G. (1971–1972). On trying to understand scientific genius. *American Scholar, 41,* 102.

HOWES, C., JAMES, J. & RITCHIE, S. (2003). Pathways to effective teaching. *Early Childhood Research Quarterly, 18* (1).

HUDLEY, C. & FRIDAY, J. (1996) Attribution bias and reactive aggression. *American Journal of Preventative Medicine, 12,* 75–81.

HUESMANN, L. R. & ERON, L. D. (1983). *Factors Influencing the Effects of Television on Children: Learning from Television: Psychological and Educational Research.* Academic Press.

HUESMANN, L. R., ANDERSON, C. A., BERKOWITZ, et al. (2001). *Media violence and the youth violence* (summary). In D. Elliot (ed.) youth violence: a report of the Surgeon General. Washington, DC: US Government Printing Office.

HUESMANN, L. R. & SKORIC, M. (2003). *Regulating media violence: Why, how, and by whom?* In B. Young & E. Palmer (Ed.) Children and the Faces of Televisual Media: Teaching, Violence, Selling. Mahwah, NJ: Lawrence Erlbaum.

HUNT, D. E. (1987). *Beginning with ourselves: In practice, theory, and human affairs.* Cambridge, MA: Brookline Books.

HYMAN, I., & SNUCK, P. A. (2001). Dangerous schools, alienated students. Reclaiming Children and Youth, 10 (3), 133–136.

JEFFREY, K. (2002). Therapeutic restraint of Children: it must always be justified. *Pediatric Nursing, 14* (9), 20–22.

JELLIFFE, D. B. (1965). Affected malnutrition on behavioral and social development. In *Proceedings of the Western Hemisphere Nutrition Congress.* Chicago, IL: American Medical Association.

JENSEN, P. S., BHATARA, V .S., VITIELLO, B., HOAGWOOD, K., FEIL, M. & BURKE, L. (1999). Psychoactive Medication Prescribing Practices for US Children: Gaps between Research and Clinical Practice. *Journal of the American Academy of Child & Adolescent Psychiatry, 38* (5), 557–565.

JOHNSON, L. (1999). The use of child-centered play therapy and filial therapy with Head Start families: a brief report. *J Marital Family Therapy. 1999 Apr; 25* (2):169–76.

Joint Commission Resources. (2000). *Restraint in behavioral health care: minimizing use, improving outcomes.* (Videotape). JCR Tape Library. Oakbrook Terrace, IL: Joint Commission Resources, Inc.

JONES, R., & TIMBERS, G. (2002). And analysis of the restraint event and its behavioral effects on clients and staff. *Reclaiming Children and Youth, 11* (1), 37–41.

JOURNAL OF SAFE MANAGEMENT. (2000). Protecting kids in restraint. *Reclaiming Children and Youth, 10* (3), 162–163.

KAGAN, S. (2001) Teaching for Character and Community. *Educational Leadership, 59* (2), 50–55.

KAPLAN, E. L. & MAYER, P. (1958). Nonparametric estimation from incomplete observations. *Journal of American Statistics, 53*:457–481.

KASTNER, J. W. (1998). Clinical Change in Adolescent Aggressive Behavior: a Group Therapy Approach. *Journal of Child and Adolescent Group Therapy, 8* (1), 23–33.

KAZDIN, A. E. (1987) *Problem-solving and parent management in treating aggressive antisocial behavior.* In E.D. Hobbs &P.S. Jensen (Eds.) Psychological treatments for child and adolescent disorder: empirically based strategies for clinical practice (pp. 377–408). Washington, DC: American Psychological Association.

KESSLER, R. C., MERIKANGAS K. R., BERGLUND, P., DEMLER, O., JIN, R. & WALTERS, E. E. (2004). Lifetime Prevalence and Age-of-Onset Distributions of DSM-IV Disorders and the National Comorbidity Survey Replication. *International Journal of Psychiatric Methods Research, 13,* 60–68.

KLEIN, S. B. (1987) *Learning: Principles and applications*. New York: McGraw-Hill, Inc.

KOOP, E. & LEEPER, B. (1992). Violence: A national emergency. *American Journal of Public Health.*

KRUESI, M. J., HIBBS, E. D., ZAHN, T. P., KEYSOR, C. S., HAMBURGER, S. D., BARTKO, J. J. & RAPOPORT, J. L. (1993). A 2-year prospective follow-up study of children and adolescents with disruptive behavior disorders. Prediction by cerebrospinal fluid 5-hydroxyindoleacetic acid, homovanillic acid, and autonomic measures? *Child Psychiatry, 30* (6), 605–614.

LAHEY, APPLEGATE, B., BERKELEY, R. A., GARFINKEL, B., MCBURNETT, K., KERDYK, L., GREENHILL, L., HYND, G. W., FRICK, P. J., & NEWCORN, J. (1994). DSM-IV field trials for oppositional defiant disorder and Condit disorder in children and adolescents. *American Journal of Psychiatry, 151,* 1163–1171.

LARSEN, E. (2003). Frontiers in strength-based treatment. *Reclaiming Children and Youth, 12* (1), 12–17.

LARSON, S. & BRENDTRO, L. (2000) *Reclaiming Our Prodigal Sons and Daughters: A practical approach for connecting with youth in conflict.* Bloomington, IN: National Education Service.

LINEHAN, M. M. (1994). The Empirical Basis of Dialectical Behavior Therapy: Development of New Treatments Versus Evaluation of Existing Treatments. *The Journal of Mind and Behavior, 15* (4), 323–342.

LIPSEY, M. W., & WILSON, D. B. (1998). *Effective intervention for serious juvenile offenders: a synthesis of research.* In R. Lobar & D. Farington (Eds.) Serious and Violent Juvenile Offenders: Risk Factors and Successful Interventions (313–345). Thousand Oaks: Sage.

LEE, C. C. (1995) *Counseling for Diversity: A guide for school counselors and related professionals.* Massachusetts: Allyn and Bacon.

LEIBERMAN, M. D. (2000). Intuition: A social cognitive neuroscience approach. *Psychological Bulletin, 126,* 109–137.

LEIBERMAN, M. D., OCHSNER, K. N., GILBERT, D. T., & SCHACTER, D. L. (2001). Do amnesics exhibit cognitive dissonance reduction? The role of explicit memory and attention in attitude change. *Psychological Science, 12,* 135–140.

LEVY, F., HAY, D. A., BENNETT, K. S. & MCSTEPHEN, M.B. (2005). Gender Differences in ADHD Subtype Comorbidity. *Journal of the American Academy of Child & Adolescent Psychiatry, 44* (4), 368–376.

LEWIS, M. V. (2000). Reformulated Attention-Deficit Hyperactivity Disorder According to Signal Detection Theory. *Journal of the American Academy of Child Psychiatry, 39* (numeral mind), 1144–1151.

LITTLE, P. F. B. (2004). Peer coaching as a support to collaborative teaching. *Mentoring and Tutoring, 13* (1), 83–94.

LOEBER, R., BURKE, J. D., LAHEY, B. B., WINTERS, A. &ZERA, M. (2000). Oppositional defined and Condit disorder: a review of the past 10 years, part I. *Journal of the American Academy of Child and Adolescent Psychiatry, 39,* 1468–1484.

LOBLEY, K. J, BEDDELEY, A. D. & GATHERCOLE, S. E. (2005). Phonological similarity effects and verbal complex span. *Psychology Press, 58* (8), 1462–1478.

LOCKMAN, J. E. & DUNN, S. E. (1993) An intervention and consultation model from a social cognitive perspective: a description of the anger-coping program. *School Psychology Review, 22,* 458–471.

LONG, N. J. (1997). The Therapeutic Power of Kindness. *Reclaiming Children and Youth, 5* (4), 242–246.

LONGHURST, J., BERKEY, L., & KEYES, B. (2001). Bully-proofing: What one district learned about improving school climate. *Reclaiming Children and Youth, 9* (4), 224–228.

LOTT, I. T., MCGREGOR, M., ENGELMAN, L., TOUCHETTE, P., TOUMAY, A., SANDMAN, C., FERNANDEZ, G., PLON, L. & WALSH, D. (2004). Longitudinal prescribing patterns for psychoactive medications in community-based individuals with developmental disabilities: utilization of pharmacy records. *Journal of Intellectual Disability Research, 48* (6), 563.

LOVELL, C. H. (1992). Breaking the cycle of poverty. West Hartford, CT: Kumarian Press.

LYNCH, M. J. (1999). Beating a dead horse: is there any basic and peer coal evidence for the deterrent effect of imprisonment? *Crime, Law, and Social Change, 31* (4), 347–362.

MACKENZIE, D. L. & PARENT, D. (1992). Boot Camp Prisons for Young Offenders. *Smart Sentencing: the Emergence of Intermediate Sanctions.* Newberry Park, CA: Sage Publications.

MACKENZIE, D. L. & HERBERT, E. E. (Eds.) (1996). *Correctional Boot Camps: a Tough Intermediate Sanction.* Washington, DC: National Institute of Justice.

MACKENZIE, D. L. (1997). Criminal Justice and Crime Prevention. In L. W. Sherman et al. (Eds.) *Preventing Crime: at What Works, What Doesn't, What's Promising (a Report to the United States Congress).* College Park, MD: Department of Criminology and Criminal Justice, University Of Maryland.

MACKENZIE, D. L., STYVE, G. J., GOVER, A. R., & WILSON, DB (2001). The Impact of Boot Camps and Traditional Institutions on Juvenile Residence: Adjustment, Perception of the Environment and Changes in Social Bonds, Impulsivity, and Antisocial Attitudes. *Journal on Research in Crime & Delinquency, 38,* 279–313.

MARGOLIN, G. & GORDIS, E. B. (2004). Children's Exposure to Violence in the Family and Community. *Current Directions and Psychological Science, 13* (4), 152.

MASH, E. & JOHNSTON, C. (1983a) Parental perceptions of child behavior problems, parenting self-esteem, and mother's reported stress in younger and older hyperactive and normal children. *Journal of Consulting and Clinical Psychology, 51,* 86–99.

MASH, E. J. & HUNSLEY, J. (2005). Evidence-based Assessment of Child and Adolescent Disorders: Issues and Challenges. *Journal of Clinical Child & Adolescent Psychology, 34* (3), 362–379

MASLOW, A. (1970). Motivation and personality. New York: Harper & Row.

MASTERS, K. J., BELLONCI, C., et al. (2002). Practice parameters for the prevention and management of aggressive behavior in Child and adolescent psychiatric institutions with special reference to seclusion and restraint. *Journal of the American Academy of Child and Adolescent Psychiatry, 41,* 4–25.

MAUGHAN, B., ROWE, R., MESSER, J., GOODMAN, R. & MELTZER, H. (2004). Condit disorder and oppositional defiant disorder in a national sample: a developmental epidemiology. *Journal of Child Psychology and Psychiatry, 45,* 609.

MAYES, L. C. (1994). Neurobiology of prenatal cocaine exposure of fact on developing monoamine systems. *Infant Mental Health Journal, 15* (2), 121–133.

MCDERMOT, B. M. & GIBBON, P. (2002). Embedding categorical constructs in contemporary Child mental health approaches. *Australian and New Zealand Journal of Psychiatry, 36* (4), 481.

MCMAHON, R. J. & SLOUGH, N. M. (1996) Family-based intervention in the FAST Track program. In: Peters R. V., MCMAHON, R. J., editors. *Preventing Childhood Disorders, Substance Abuse and Delinquency.* California: Sage, pp 298–328.

MESULAM, M. M., JOHNSON, N., GRUJIC, J. & WEINTRAUB, S.: Apolipoprotein E genotypes in primary progressive aphasia. *Neurology 49:* 51–55, 1997.

MILNE, J. (2001) Family treatment of Oppositional Defiant Disorder: Changing views and strength-based approaches. *Family Journal, 9.*

MORASH, M. & RUCKER, L. (1990). A Critical Look at the Idea of Boot Camp As a Correctional Reform. *Crime & Delinquency, 36,* 204–222.

MPOFU, E. & CRYSTAL, R. (2001) Conduct disorder in children: Challenges, and prospective cognitive behavioural treatments. *Counseling Psychology Quarterly, 14.*

MULLEN, J. K. (2000). The physical restraint controversy. *Reclaiming Children and Youth, 9* (2), 92–94, 124.

MURRAY, J. P. (2001) TV violence and brain mapping and children. *Psychiatric Times 18* (10).

NARAIN, C. (2006) Childhood Developmental Disorders. *Nature Neuroscience 9,* 1209.

NEWCORN, J. H., SPENCER, T. J., BEIDERMAN, J., MILTON, D. & MICHELSON, D. (2005). Atomoxetine Treatment in Children and Adolescents with Attention-Deficit/Hyperactivity Disorder and Comorbid Oppositional Defiant Disorder. *Journal of the American Academy of Child & Adolescent Psychiatry, 44* (3), 240, 248.

NICKEL, M. K., KRAWCZYK, J., NICKEL, C., FORTHUBER, P., KETTLER, C., LEIBERICH, P., MUELBACHER, M., TRITT, K., MITTERLEHNER, F. O., LAHMANN, C., ROTHER, W. K. & LOEW, T. H. (2005). Anger, Interpersonal Relationships, and Health-Related Quality of Life in Bullying Boys Who Are Treated with Outpatient Family Therapy: a Randomized, Prospective, Controlled Trial with 1 Year of Follow-Up. *Pediatrics, 116* (2), 247–254.

NIJSTAD, B. A., STROEBE, W. & LODEWIJKX, H.F.M. (2003). Production blocking an idea generation: does blocking interfere with cognitive processes? *Journal of Experimental Social Psychology, 39* (6), 531–548.

NISBETT, R. & WILSON, T. (1977). Telling more than we can know: Verbal reports on mental processes. *Psychological Review, 84,* 231–259.

OESTERREICH, L. (1995). Ages & stages-five-year-olds. Oesterreich, L., Holt, B. & Karas, S., *Iowa family child care handbook*, 207–210. Ames, IA: Iowa State University Extension.

OESTERREICH, L. (1995). Ages & stages- six through eight -year-olds. Oesterreich, L., Holt, B. & Karas, S., *Iowa family child care handbook*, 211–212. Ames, IA: Iowa State University Extension.

OLVERA, R. L. (2002). Intermittent explosive disorder: epidemiology, diagnosis and management. *Central Nervous System Drugs, 16,* 517–526.

ORTIZ, J. & RAINE, A. D. (2004). Heart Rate Level and Antisocial Behavior in Children and Adolescents: a Meta-Analysis. *Journal of the American Academy of Child & Adolescent Psychiatry, 43* (2), 154–162.

OZSIVADJIAN, A. (2008) Cognitive Behaviour Therapy for Children and Families. *Journal of Applied Research in Intellectual Disabilities 21* (1) , 100–101.

PS026610, PS026611, PS026612. NATIONAL TELEVISION VIOLENCE STUDY. Volumes 1, 2, and 3. Margaret Seawell, Ed. 1997.

PAPPADOPULOS, E., MACINTYRE, J. C., CRISMON, ML, et al. (2003). Treatment recommendations for the use of antipsychotics for aggressive youth. Part II. *Journal of the American Academy of Child and Adolescent Psychiatry, 42* (2), 145–161

PATTERSON, G. R. & FORGATCH, M. S. (1987) *Parents and Adolescents Living Together.* Oregon: Castalia.

PETTI, L. et al (2003). Perception of Nonverbal Emotion Cues by Children with Nonverbal Learning Disabilities. *Journal of Developmental and Physical Disabilities, Volume 15,* Number 1, March.

POLLIT, E. & THOMSON, C. (1977). Protein-calorie malnutrition and behavior: a view from psychology. In *Nutrition and the brain*, 2 (Eds.) R.J. Wurthman & J.J. Wurthman. New York: Raven Press.

PROVENCO, E. (1991). *Videogame Kids: Making Sense of Nintendo.* Harvard University Press.

QUIGLEY, R. (2003). The colorful evolution of a strength-based treatment model. *Reclaiming Children and Youth, 12* (1), 28–32.

RADIGAN, M., LANNON, P., ROOHAN, P. & GESTEN, F. (2005). Medication Patterns for Attention-Deficit/Hyperactivity Disorder and Comorbid Psychiatric Conditions in a Low-Income Population. *Journal of Child and Adolescent Psychopharmacology, 15* (1), 44–56.

RATNER, C. (1993 a). A socio-historical approach to contextualism. In S. Hayes, L. Hayes, h. Reese, & T. Sarbin (Eds.), *Varieties of scientific contextualism* (169–186). Reno: Context Press.

RAY, D. C. (2006). Evidence Based Play Therapy. *Contemporary Play Therapy: Theory, Research, and Practice.* Guilford Press.

RAYCHABA, B. (1982). Commentary-"Out of control": A Youth perspective unsecured treatments and physical restraint. *Journal of Child and Youth Care, 7,* 83–87.

REGIER, D. A., KAELBER, C. T., RAE, D. S., FARMER, M. E., KNAUPER, B., KESSLER, R. C. & NORQUIST, G. S. (1998). Limitations of diagnostic criteria and assessment instruments for mental disorders: implications for research and policy. *Archives of General Psychiatry, 55,* 109–115.

RODICK, A. (Ed.) (2003). *A revolution in kindness.* West Sussex, UK: Anita Roddick Books.

ROGERS, S. J., WHENER, E. A. & HAGERMAN, R. (2001). The Behavioral Phenotype in Fragile X: Symptoms of Autism in Very Young Children with Fragile X Syndrome, Idiopathic Autism, and Other Developmental Disorders. *Journal of Developmental & Behavioral Pediatrics, 22* (6), 409–417.

ROLLIN, S. A., KAISER-ULREY, C., POTTS, I. & CREASON, A. H. (2003). A school-based violence prevention model for at-risk eighth-grade youth. *Psychology in the Schools, 40* (4), 403–416.

ROSENBERG, M. (1999). *Nonviolent communication.* Encinitas, CA: Puddle Dancer Press.

ROSS, C. & BLANC, H. (2000) Parenting stress in mothers of young children with Oppositional Defiant Disorder and other severe behavior disorders. *Child Study Journal, 28.*

ROTHEREM-BORUS, M. J. & DUAN, N. (2003). Generation of preventative interventions. *Child and Adolescent Psychiatry, 42* (5), 518–526.

SAPER, B. (1971). Psycho-Economic Reinforcement As Treatment. *Psychiatric Quarterly, 45* (3), 458–462.

SCAHILL, L. & SCHWAB-STONE, M. (2000). Epidemiology of ADHD and school-age children. *Child and Adolescent Psychiatric Clinic North America, 9,* 541–555.

SCHEFF, T. J. (2005). The Structure of Context: Deciphering Frame Analysis. *Sociological Theory 23* (4), 368–385.

SCHOLTE, E. M. (1992). Prevention and treatment of juvenile problem behavior: a proposal for a socio-ecological approach. *Journal of Abnormal Child Psychology, 20* (3), 247–262.

SCHWARTZ, B. (1978) *Psychology of Learning and Behavior.* New York: W.W. Norton and Company, Inc.

SCREIER, H. (2001) Socially Awkward Children: Neurocognitive Contributions. *Psychiatric Times, Vol. XVII,* Issue 9.

SECHREST, D. D. (1989). *Prison "Boot Camps" Do Not Measure up.* Federal Probation, 53, 15–20.

SEITA, J. & BRENDTRO, L. (2002). *Kids who outwit adults.* Long Mount, CO: Sopris West.

SELLS, S. P. (1998). *Treating the tough adolescent.* New York: The Guilford Press.

SERKETICH, W. J. & DUMAS, J. E. (1996) The effectiveness of behavioral parent training to modify antisocial behavior in children: A meta-analysis. *Behavior Therapy, 27,* 159–170.

SEIGELMAN, C. & MANSFIELD, K. (1992) Knowledge of and receptivity to psychological treatment in childhood and adolescence. *Journal of Clinical Child Psychology, 21,* 2–9.

SOLNICK, J., BRAUKMANN, C., BEDLINGTON, M., KIRIGIN, K. & WOLFE, M. (1981). The relationship between parent-youth interaction and delinquency in group homes. *Journal of Abnormal Child Psychology, 9* (1), 107–119.

SILVERMAN, W. (2003). Using CBT in the Treatment of Social Phobia, Separation Anxiety and GAD. *Psychiatric Times, September, Vol. XX,* Issue 9.

SKINNER, B. F. (1969) *Contingencies of Reinforcement: A Theoretical Analysis.* New York: Meredith Corporation.

SNYDER. B.A. (1997). Expressive Art Therapy Techniques: Healing the Soul through Creativity. *Journal of Humanistic Education and Development, v36 n2 p74–82,* Dec.

SOBEL, D. M., TENENBAUM, J. B. & GOPNIK, A. (2004). Children's causal references from indirect evidence: backwards blocking and Bayesian reasoning in preschoolers. *Cognitive Science: a Multidisciplinary Journal, 28* (3), 303–333.

SOLNICK, J., BRAUKMANN, C., BEDLINGTON, M., KIRIGIN, K. & WOLFE, M. (1981). The relationship between parent-youth interaction and delinquency in group homes. *Journal of Abnormal Child Psychology, 9* (1), 107-119.

STALLER, J. A., WADE, M. J. & BAKER, M. (2005). Current Prescribing Patterns in Outpatient Child and Adolescent Psychiatric Practice in Central New York. *Journal of Child and Adolescent Psychopharmacology, 15* (1), 57–61.

STEIN, J., et al (2002). In harm's way: toxic threats to child development. *Journal of Dev Beh Pediatric. 23* (1): S13–22.

STOCK, G. (1988) *The Kid's Book of Questions.* New York: Workman Publishing.

STORMSHACK, E. (2000) Parenting practices and child disruptive behavior problems in early elementary school. *Journal of Clinical Psychology, 29.*

STYVE, G. J., MACKENZIE, D. L., GOVER, A. R. & MITCHELL, O. (2000). Perceived Conditions of Confinement: a National of Valuation of Juvenile Boot Camps and Traditional Facilities. *Law and Human Behavior, 24* (3), 297–308.

TEASDALE, J.D., et al (2003)Mindfulness Training and Problem Formulation, *Clinical Psychology: Science and Practice 10* (2), 157–160.

THOMPSON, C. L. & RUDOLPH, L. B. (1996) *Counseling Children* (Fourth Edition). Pacific Grove, CA: Brooks/Cole Publishing.

THOMPSON, T. & GRABOWSKI, J. G. (1972) *Reinforcement Schedules and Multi-operant Analysis.* New York: Meredith Corporation.

TIWARI, S., PODELL, J.C., MARTIN, E.D., MYCHAILYSZYN, M.P., FURR, J.M. & KENDALL, P.C. (2008). Experiential avoidance in the parenting of anxious youth: Theory, research, and future directions. *Cognition and Emotion, 1,* 26–35.

TREMBLAY, R. E., VITARO, F., BERTRAND, L., LEBLANC, M., BEAUCHESNE, H. & BIOLEAU, H. (1992) Parent and child training to prevent early onset of delinquency: the Montreal longitudinal study. In: MCCORD, J. & TREMBLAY, R. E. (Eds.) *Parenting Antisocial Behavior: Interventions From Birth Through Adolescence.* New York: Guilford.

TRIESCHMAN, A. E., WHITAKER, J. K. & BRENDTRO, L. K. (1969). *The other 23 hours.* New York: Aldine de Gruyter.

TSAL, Y., SHALEV, L. & MEVORACH, C. (2005). The diversity of attention deficits in ADHD: the prevalence of four cognitive factors and ADHD versus controls. *Journal of Learning Disability, 38* (2), 142–157.

TURKLE, S. (1984). *The Second Self: Computers and the Human Spirit.* London: Granada.

VANDERVEN, K. (2000). Cultural aspects of point and level systems. *Reclaiming Children and Youth, 9* (1), 53–59.

VAN DE WIEL, N., VAN GOOZEN, S., MATTHYS, W., SNOEK, H., & VAN ENGELAND, H. (2004). Cortisol and Treatment Effect in Children with Disruptive Behavior Disorders: A Preliminary Study. *Journal of the American Academy of Child & Adolescent Psychiatry, 43* (8), 1011–1018.

VAN DER KOLK, B. A. & VAN DER HART, O. (1991) The intrusive past: The flexibility of memory and the engraving of trauma. *American Imago: 48:* 425–454.

VAN DER KOLK, B. A., DUCEY, C. P. (1989) The psychological processing of traumatic experience: Rorschach patterns in PTSD. *Journal of Traumatic Stress, 2:* 259–274.

VAN DER KOLK, B. A., PERRY, J. C., HERMAN, J. L. (1991) Childhood origins of self- destructive behavior. *American Journal of Psychiatry, 148:* 1665–1671.

VLADIN, S. (2006). Anxiety states: a review of conceptual and treatment issues. Personality disorders and neuroses. *Current Opinion in Psychiatry. 19* (1) :79–83, January.

VORRATH, H. H. & BRENDTRO, L. K. (1974). *Positive peer culture.* New York: Aldine de Gruyter. Second edition published 1985.

WEAKLAND, J., FISH, R., WATZLAWICK, P. & BODIN, A. (1974). Brief therapy: Focused problem resolution. *Family Process, 13,* 141–168.

WEAKLAND, J. (1976) Communication therapy and clinical change. In: GUERIN, P. (Ed.) *Family Therapy* (pp 111–128). New York: Gardener.

WEEMS, C. F., SALTZMAN, K. M., REISS, A. L. & CARRION, V. G. (2003). A prospective test of the association between hyper or arousal and emotional numbing in youth with a history of traumatic stress. *Journal of Clinical Child and Adolescent Psychology, 32* (1), 166–171.

WEISSENBERGER, A. A., DELL, M. L., LIOW, K., THEODORE, W., FRATTALI, C. M., HERNANDEZ, D. & ZAMETKIN, A. (2001). Aggression and Psychiatric Comorbidity and Children with Hypothalamus Hamartomas and Their Unaffected Siblings. *Journal of the American Academy of Child & Adolescent Psychiatry, 40* (6), 696–703.

WELLS, A. (2002). GAD, Meta-cognition, and Mindfulness: An Information Processing Analysis. *Clinical Psychology: Science and Practice 9* (1), 95–100.

WERTSCH, J. (1985 a). *Culture, communication, and cognition: Vygotskian perspectives.* New York: Cambridge University Press.

WILENS, T. E., SPENCER, T. J., BEIDERMAN, J & SCHLEIFER, D. (1997). Case study: Nefazodone for Juvenile Mood Disorders. *Journal of the American Academy of Child & Adolescent Psychiatry, 36* (4), 481–485.

WILSON, J. (2005). Boot camps and effectiveness. *American Journal of Psychiatry, 161,* 184.

WINNER, M. (2002). *Thinking About You Thinking About Me.* San Jose, CA: Author.

WOCOLDO, C. (2006). Social skills and nonverbal decoding of emotions in very preterm children at early school age. *Psychology Press, Volume 3,* Number 1.

WOLIN, S. (2003). What is a strength? *Reclaiming Children and Youth, 12* (1), 18–21.

RIGHT, S. (1999). Physical restraint in the management of violence and aggression in in-patient settings: a review of issues. *Journal of Mental Health, 8* (5), 459–472.

YALOM, I. D. (2002) *The Gift of Therapy,* New York: HarperCollins Publishers.

YALOM, I. D. & YALOM, B. (Ed.) (1998) *The Yalom Reader: Selections From the Work of A Master Therapist and Storyteller.* New York: Perseus Books.

YALOM, I. D. (1995) *The Theory and Practice of Group Psychotherapy* (Fourth Edition). New York: Basic Books

YATES, A. J. (1975) *Theory and Practice in Behavior Therapy.* Canada: John Wiley & Sons, Inc.

ZAHN, T. P. & KRUESI, M. J. (1993). Autonomic activity and boys with disruptive behavior disorders. *Psychophysiology, 33* (4), 612–628.

ZILLMAN, D. (1993). Mental control of angry aggression. In D. M. WEGNER & J. W. PENEBAKER (Eds.), *Handbook of mental control* (370–392). Upper Saddle River, New Jersey: Prentice-Hall.